WHAT ABOUT
TEEN-AGE MARRIAGE?

WHAT ABOUT TEEN-AGE MARRIAGE?

by Jeanne Sakol

Foreword by Dr. Rebecca Liswood, Executive Director, Marriage Counseling Service of Greater New York.

Julian Messner, Inc.   New York

Published by Julian Messner, Inc.
8 West 40 Street, New York 18

Published simultaneously in Canada
by The Copp Clark Publishing Co. Limited

Printed in the United States of America
Library of Congress Catalog Card No. 61-7998

We are grateful to the following for permission to quote from the following media:

From LOVE AND MARRIAGE by F. Alexander Magoun. Reprinted by permission of Harper & Brothers.

From "The Private Lives of Teen-Agers" by Max Lerner in the New York Post. Copyright 1958, New York Post Corporation. Reprinted by permission of the New York Post Corporation.

From BOY MARRIES GIRL by Kenneth L. Cannon and Hazel Anthony. Reprinted by permission of Oxford Book Company, Inc.

From "Premarital Counseling" by Eleanor Hamilton, Ph.D. in Modern Bride. Reprinted by permission of Dr. Eleanor Hamilton.

FOREWORD

As a Marriage Counselor keenly interested in helping young people attain a healthier and more adult interpersonal relationship in marriage, I am happy to recommend Jeanne Sakol's book, WHAT ABOUT TEEN-AGE MARRIAGE?

This book deals with the problems that teen-agers are faced with from many different points of view and in many different areas. The author knows teen-agers—she knows that they want the facts stated honestly and directly, and her straight-from-the-shoulder approach has a freshness that is just right for her audience.

While the book is directed to girls, boys will benefit from it since they are, after all, the second party to the important subject of marriage. Parents too should read this book to gain a more realistic attitude in handling the various problems that teen-agers face today.

Rebecca Liswood, M. D.

CONTENTS

PREFACE

This is a personal book; personal to all teen-agers who may be thinking about marriage; personal to their families and friends who want them to make the right decisions; and personal to me, too, because I have a fourteen-going-on-fifteen-year-old sister, Phyllis, who has just started thinking about marriage. Not about *getting* married, of course, but she is getting interested in the whole exciting business of meeting boys, falling in love, getting married, leaving home and having babies in the not too distant future.

A lot of my ideas for this book came from private gab sessions with Phyllis, stretched out on the floor of her bedroom, playing records and doing our nails. In these sister-to-sister talks, she wanted to know about falling in love, having crushes—about whether you feel different after you're married, and also about more practical things like how much it costs to have a baby.

Remembering the curiosity and bewilderment of my own teens and the sudden, terrible need for someone my own age to love and understand me, I enjoyed discussing these things openly and frankly and decided to write a straightforward, realistic book covering all aspects of teen-age marriage: the physical responsibilities of marital love and childbearing; the emotional upset on leaving home and accepting the maturity of marriage; the social differences that come with marriage; the financial side of housekeeping.

Not being a professional marriage expert, I have spent many months studying what the leading authorities have to say, poring through surveys, reading case histories, tracking down statistics on the successes and failures of early marriage. What you may gain. What you give up. The advantages and drawbacks, privileges and responsibilities. I have tried to answer all possible questions and present a clear, unprejudiced view of what happens when you trade in your school ring for a wedding ring.

WHAT ABOUT TEEN-AGE MARRIAGE? takes no sides. Neither for nor against, it takes the view that every teen-ager is a distinctly individual person. While many may dress alike, laugh at the same jokes, hang out together and seem the same, some may be ready for early marriage while others should wait a bit.

Whether or not you're ready is one of the most far-reaching decisions of your life. Even the great philosopher Diogenes said, "Whichever you do, you may regret it."

So let's talk about teen-age marriage and perhaps it will help you to a deeper understanding of yourself as a person and of your future as a partner in marriage.

WHAT ABOUT
TEEN-AGE MARRIAGE?

1

IS IT LOVE—OR SEX?

Love is probably the most overused word in the English language. In quick succession, you can "love" pickles, Elvis, the new kitchen curtains and beach parties. Then, quite suddenly, you will find a new meaning for love when you meet some one special person.

Then, watch out! When this new kind of love happens, the other loves fade into oblivion. This is the real thing! Love with a capital L!

How can you be sure? Easy. The proof is all there. The mere thought of this other person gives you goose pimples. You're not sick but you get hot and cold all over. You may not be able to eat a thing, or you may wolf your way through a whole chocolate cake without knowing you're doing it.

The telephone and doorbell are electric shocks charging up your backbone and catapulting you into delirium. It takes you hours to get dressed, hours to fall asleep. You feel drunk, giddy, jet-propelled, way above all earthly cares, cut off from everyone and everything except THE ONE.

While all this is going on, current pop songs, love stories, movies, TV and the romance magazines seem to have been created *for* you, *about* you, dramatizing *your* unbearably wonderful feelings. *NO. IT's PROBABLY DEXEDRINE*

But is it really love? Or are you just feeling the sexual changes in your body which come with the growth from childhood to adulthood. While it is possible to be beautifully and genuinely in love in your early teens—and many successful marriages begin as crushes —often what is thought to be love is pure and simple sexual attraction, or infatuation. Nature is pretty sly about the Mating Instinct. In order for life to go on generation after generation, living things must reproduce. In order to reproduce the species, there must be an inner drive toward mating with the opposite sex.

Millions of words have been written, sung, sighed, moaned and groaned about love, but very few have really defined what love actually is. Among the best is, "Love is a Mutual Admiration Society," said by Dr. Rebecca Liswood, Executive Director of the Marriage Counseling Service of Greater New York. "Love should build you up, never tear you down. Love enables you to criticize less, sympathize more!"

Also of value, M.I.T. Professor F. A. Magoun wrote, "Love is the feeling of security and contentment that comes with the satisfaction of each person's emotional needs through their mutual efforts. Love produces a kinship of body, mind and spirit."

Therefore, if you believe you are smiling into the face of Love, be sure you see Mutual Admiration, Genuine Sympathy, Emotional Security and a Sense of Contentment before you accept it as the real thing.

Adolescence brings with it a delicious, if sometimes mystifying, awakening of body functions. It's important to recognize that physically you are ready and able to mate and have babies. Your glands and reproductive organs are ready to function and the yearnings you have are Nature's way of saying, "Let's go!"

This is where the trouble sometimes starts. According to sociologist Evelyn Duvall, "During the teens, sex powers reach full development. There is often an urgency for sex expression that is hard to control. The dilemma becomes a baffling one. Young people today have far more freedom than in former years. A young person's conduct is largely a personal responsibility. Parents no longer choose one's mate or closely supervise one's courting. Young people are more frequently exposed to potential danger and, unless adequately prepared to meet it wisely, are more often likely to make mistakes."

Sexual desire is like the rope in a tug-o'-war with Right and Wrong pulling hard in opposite directions. The questions to ask yourself are these: Do I control my body or does my body control me? Do I understand my body and recognize how it can make my future marriage happy and provide healthy children? Or will I submit to the physical reaction that sweeps me into unfortunate situations which I know will lead to trouble?

In discussing the "animal urge," Dr. Mary Macaulay says, "In human beings, as in the rest of the animal kingdom, the biological purpose of sex is procreation of young for the continuity of the race. If it were not for the sexual urge, the human race would die out. It is therefore interesting to understand a little of how our bodies work and the mechanism by which reproduction is carried on."

Animal instinct and sexual urges notwithstanding, the fact remains that infatuation and physical attraction are part of being in love, so how can you tell whether your feelings are deep and lasting?

Here is a "Love or Sex?" Quiz which may help you to understand.

"IS IT LOVE—OR SEX?"

Answer each question honestly, Yes or No. An analysis of your answers follows:

1. If he doesn't have a car and can't borrow his father's, are you restless because you can't go anywhere?

2. Do you feel angry if he has to study or work and can't see you?

3. Are you frantic if another girl pays attention to him?

4. Is love-making the most important part of your times together?

5. Are you just the least bit sorry for him?

6. What about the things you don't like. Do you think your love will reform him?

7. Have you the same ideas about money?

8. Do you ever spend an evening together without necking?

9. Is he the answer to all your problems?

10. Can you see him as the father of your children?

WHAT YOUR ANSWERS MAY MEAN:

1. If the answer is YES and you are restless without transportation—and the privacy of a car—then chances are you are infatuated. Being in love means the ability to enjoy his company whatever you're doing, or not doing. This is a severe test but one which always works.

If you can be happy and companionable "doing nothing," this is one solid sign of true love.

2. Loving him, you would be sorry not to see him, but if you were angry it would show that your feelings were selfish in wanting him to dance attendance regardless of his other responsibilities. Loving means helping, not demanding.

3. Possessiveness is a primitive emotion and is generally aroused by feelings of sexual attraction rather than love. Tearing somebody's hair out in the ladies room may sound highly romantic, but jealous outbursts are the most superficial expressions of feeling. Remember that girls are naturally more possessive than boys and if you truly love him you will want others to meet him, talk to him, discover just how great he is.

4. If you have very little to say to each other and can't wait until you can park somewhere quiet, or until your family has gone to sleep so you can have the living room, then you must give some serious thought to what's going on. What happens many times is this—two people meet, have lots in common, feel a strong attraction and "fall in love." Only, gradually their mutual interests fade and, without realizing it, the only thing that keeps them together is sex.

5. Sympathy and compassion are valuable traits. They help to make you a good friend, an aware member of society. But don't mistake them for love. Helping someone, listening to someone's problems, understand-

ing him are all worthwhile but don't confuse them with being in love.

6. The biggest mistake you can make is playing The Reformer. If he's lazy, you can't hold his nose to the grindstone. If he tells little white lies to others, don't think you're going to be exempt or that your affection is going to change him. Being in love means no self-delusion. If you can face all his faults and still love him, you need look no further.

7. Money, however crude it may sound, is important to love. Some of us spend money foolishly, never worrying or caring whether or not we have it. Others have been taught to save some, spend some. Differences in attitude toward money can be the source of great unhappiness. Mutual understanding is one of the basic parts of love and if you can't see eye to eye on money your chances of happiness are remote.

8. When necking and petting become part of the social pattern, like having a hamburger, you are dissipating one of the deepest and most rewarding pleasures of love. Necking is demeaning to love, puts it in the same category as eating too much rich food every day, which can spoil your appetite completely. While love-making is one way couples show their feelings, neither of you should feel you must neck or pet at every meeting in order to prove your affection. If constant "proof" is necessary then the basic trust and understanding that go with real love are sadly missing.

9. "Nobody understands me," you may say. And

you're probably right. The teen age brings with it physical and emotional change. Every few months brings new yearnings, new worries as well as new realizations. You're bubbling over with all sorts of conflicts and until you simmer down, your family, your teachers— even you yourself—will have a tough time understanding you. So naturally when some one person turns up who seems to know what you're thinking before you think it, to sense when you're shy, to say the right thing at the right time, surely this must be the one for you. You may be right. Instinctive sympathy and harmony are vital to happiness. But don't allow one person to be your barrier against the world. Even if it develops that you are in love and will marry, you must still be a part of the community and have mutual understanding with others.

10. Having children is the fundamental desire of every girl. Part of your love for a man is visualizing him as your future protector and the father of your offspring. If you can think of your boy friend only as a fabulous dancer or terrific driver or very cute looking, you are in love with the idea of love, not with him.

There's no score for this little quiz. You know yourself what your answers reveal. One point I'd like to make is if you have discovered that your feelings at the moment seem honestly to be Sex instead of Love— don't worry! Feeling sexual attraction and needs are natural. These feelings are not wrong. What is wrong is feeling *guilty* about them, and instead of facing up to the responsibility of adult urges and controlling them, you may convince yourself that sexual feelings are "dirty" but that if you are in love, it's okay.

Partly to blame for this fairy tale approach are the movies where boy and girl meet, their eyes light up like pinball machines, firecrackers go off and they hot-rod into the sunset together.

You have a far better chance of recognizing true and lasting love if you face the facts of sex. You will also avoid the terrible disappointment that comes when the kick is gone and you're kicking yourself for spoiling everything, though you don't know why. Accept the fact that you will be attracted to the opposite sex the way bees are to honey. Remember, too, that even when you find deep and lasting love, you may still find others attractive, that this animal instinct response will not mean you have fallen out of love—unless you weren't in love in the first place.

According to experts K. L. Connon and Hazel Anthony, "Strong physical attraction is an important aspect of love but it would be foolish to think that that is all there is to love. As the basis for marriage, it leaves much to be desired."

Romeo and Juliet were teen-agers, but they didn't live long enough to see if their violent passion produced a happy marriage. They needed each other. They were going to "show" their parents. They impetuously defied tradition and their story has become one of the world's

25

most poignant tragedies. Yet each had a sense of personal identity. They didn't seem to feel quite as lonely as many of us feel today, though their need to cling together was just as strong.

If you can't stand on your own two feet alone, you may seem upright if somebody props you up, but you'll collapse again the minute the support is taken away. Personal identity—knowing who you are and what you want to get from life and give to it—is essential yet difficult to attain.

"If a girl pets because she can't keep the boy without petting, and because she can't date if she loses the boy, all the high-flown talk of love doesn't make a person out of her," explains Max Lerner. "Love is a difficult and complex emotion and the capacity to love and be loved is likely to be purchased at the cost of considerable grief. I have seen teen-agers so anxious to prove their love to themselves—to the world—to each other —that they run into impetuous and disastrous early marriage. I should be content if teen-agers did not aim at quite so romantic a height. I should be content if they aimed at treating each other and themselves as persons—instead of like objects waiting to be used."

What, then, is love, and how can we define it?

Love is the sum total of many things. It includes deep affection, honest admiration and a genuine feeling of true friendship. It covers tenderness, devotion and an acute awareness of the other person's fears and weaknesses. It is built on enthusiasm and stimulation. It thrives on shared interests and physical attraction.

Many teen-agers who expected love to hit them like a ton of gold-plated bricks were amazed when they discovered the down-to-earth truth.

Mary Elizabeth, seventeen, explained, "The other night, when Tod was helping me with my homework, I suddenly realized how much I *liked* him, really and truly liked him aside from loving him. I admire him, too, for his honesty and for his patience with me when I'm acting up because I'm worried about something. It's a funny thing to say about the man you love but he's the best friend I have."

Diana, at eighteen, wrote, "I knew I was in love with Pete when I found out what his sore spots are and all I could think of was how to protect him from being hurt. He's convinced he's funny looking so I don't rave about Tony Curtis or Bobby Darin because it might make him feel bad. He has two left feet on the dance floor and feels like a dope, so if he doesn't want to dance I don't make a fuss. When you love somebody, you get a new sense of what's important and what isn't."

"We knew we had found love," said seventeen-year-old Catherine, "because we both got charged up over the same things. It started with stamps. That's how we met, at the Stamp Club after school. Then, since we both like American history, we took a bicycle trip to a pioneer cabin that's been restored with all the old furniture and utensils. It was wonderful. He gave me a watch for my birthday and we've decided that if we still feel the same way about each other when Eddie graduates in June, we'll get engaged."

More poetic perhaps is the definition of love by the late Dr. Marion Hilliard, a leading adviser on human relations: "Love is the ability to accept a person just as he is. Love understands, respects and is always willing to wait. Love listens, then gives. Love is also joyful and at times exquisitely and quietly humorous. Love is more powerful than passion."

2

THE FOUR TROUBLEMAKERS:
Boredom   Jealousy   Loneliness   Fear

Everyone knows that the teens are supposed to be the happiest years of your life. They should be and could be if it weren't for The Four Troublemakers: Boredom, Jealousy, Loneliness and Fear. Each is a giant-sized agent of destruction that attacks the young and inexperienced. Each is poisonous enough to keep you from enjoying your teens and from developing into a happy adult.

Maybe you're a victim. Maybe you feel nothing ever happens to you, that whoever invented The Rut had you in mind as a tenant. School is the same old grind day after endless day. Your friends have the same old faces; they crack the same old corny jokes and play the same old phony records. Your family? They're too much, boring beyond belief, how they stand each other you'll never know. At times you're so restless and irritated you can't even stand the sight of yourself. It's that bad.

Will this excruciating boredom never end?

To begin with, what you're going through is the natural rebellion of your body that erupts during the final stages of maturity. You not only have Growing Pains but a few Growing Aches, too. You're aching to leave the nest, try your own wings, choose your own direction. You're anxious to know everything about life, sex, marriage. You want the world to treat you as the adult you've become instead of the child you were such a short time ago.

To top all this emotional chaos, you're probably going steady, maybe you're even engaged-to-be-engaged and probably your boy friend feels as you do, that life is at a standstill and you wish you were thousands of miles away where something more interesting is surely going on.

So what happens? How do you escape?

"I've got a great idea. Let's get married!" Maybe you say it. Maybe he says it. You both giggle self-consciously and then suddenly it may seem to be the one and only answer to everything.

The thrill of it all! A wedding. A honeymoon. Deciding on the kind of furniture you want, where you will live, how many children you will have.

While marriage is admittedly an exciting adventure, unlike an African safari, it's supposed to last a lifetime, to be a continuous exploration of the richness and vastness of human experience. Like any adventure, however, you must be prepared. Hillary didn't conquer Mount Everest because one fine morning he was bored and it seemed like a great idea to charge up a mountain. He planned carefully for many months, preparing himself in every way: physically—to withstand the demands on his body; emotionally—to withstand the strain of obstacles and disappointments; financially—to pay for the food, clothing and equipment necessary for ultimate success.

Of course very few people have conquered Everest and there are countless happy marriages. Yet it is as haphazard to approach marriage without forethought as it would be to start up the Himalayas without careful preparation.

So if you're listless, disinterested in things, if you feel suffocated at home, bored at school, then it's obvious that something must be done—but keep marriage as a last resort. More important, if you've been dragging around for weeks in this condition, have a medical checkup. You could easily be anemic or deficient in some vital vitamin.

What happened to a sixteen-year-old Nebraskan is a case in point. Entering her junior year at high school, Nancy had good grades, enjoyed movies and bowling, got along well with her family, her schoolmates and her steady, Bart. Yet within a few months everything changed. Her schoolwork began to fail. She "couldn't be bothered" with her favorite subjects, history and English. Movies, bowling, her family, her friends—all "bored her." Bart did everything he could to snap her out of it, even going so far as to suggest they get married.

Before she could make a decision, her father announced, "If you're so bored with life, there must be something wrong with *you*, not life. I'm taking you to the doctor."

A thorough examination showed that Nancy's trouble was simple to diagnose, simpler to cure. She needed glasses! Slightly nearsighted, her studies had become a bore because she couldn't see clearly enough to concentrate. Her bowling had suffered from faulty perspective. Not seeing properly had knocked everything out of kilter and she had retreated behind a wall of boredom.

Recalling the dreary months, Nancy said, "It was awful. Everything was too much trouble. I couldn't get worked up over anything. It was like being in a coma."

Boredom being the problem, attack the problem for what it is. Don't make the problem worse by thinking that marriage is the remedy. Marriage has enough problems of its own without having to solve an entirely different set of woes. Getting wed with the thought, "Now I can sit back and be happy," is a cordial invitation to disaster.

"The marriage of those who turn to wedlock as a cure-all for their personal problems—or as an escape from the stresses of life—is doomed at the start," states Dr. David R. Mace, a marriage counsellor for more than twenty years and staff consultant to the Marriage Council of Philadelphia.

A big point he makes is that people who succeed in marriage are those who also succeed in whatever else they undertake. A girl who can't get along with other people, who can't see a project through, who can't cope with emergencies or disappointments, is hardly someone who can handle the responsibilities of married life.

Another expert, Dr. Carney Landis, says, "No girl should marry in the hope that her marriage will solve her essential unhappiness. We have no evidence that it ever does offer such a solution and we have abundant evidence that the woman continues to be unhappy and maladjusted and adds her unhappiness to the problems of her husband."

If boredom, then, is your problem and you feel that if you don't do something right away you'll scream, my advice is—SCREAM!—as long and as loud as you please. You'll not only clear your lungs and feel a lot better but you'll find that a few primitive yelps now are better therapy than months of whimpering over why you ever got married.

Getting to the heart of boredom does not mean placidly putting up with things as they are. By all means, *do* something different to snap out of the doldrums. This is the time, when you're young and have no responsibilities except to yourself, to try new things, do new things, see new things. Change your hair style. Study ballet. Save up for a tape recorder. Visit someone you haven't seen for sometime. Be daring without being foolhardy. You can always change your hair again, trade in your ballet slippers for a xylophone, unpack your suitcase—and be more worldly for the experience.

Indulge your whims on whimsical things, be frivolous with frivolities. Save marriage for a time of serious decision, because if you decide afterward that it was all a foolish mistake—like those peppermint-stripe tights —the road back is painful if not impassable.

Asked how they beat boredom, here is what a group of girls of fifteen to eighteen said:

Allison, fifteen: "Whenever I'm bored, I cook. I bake a chocolate cake or a gooey pizza and invite my friends over to eat it. Once I tried a chocolate pizza and had to throw it out. Working in the kitchen helps my schoolwork, too. While I'm fixing things I review all that happened in class."

Jane, eighteen: "Clothes always cheer me up. I took a course at Singer Sewing so now I can remodel my clothes, change them around to look different. The last time I got disgusted with life, I took the collar off my dress coat and replaced it with a raccoon collar from a jacket. It looks very nice."

Terry, fifteen: "I was bored and so were some of the other girls, so we got together and asked our mothers if one of them would chaperon us on a weekend trip to the mountains. One mother said okay so we saved and earned extra money baby-sitting. It was the first time I ever stayed at a hotel."

Angela, sixteen: "Ever since I joined the Girl Scouts, I don't get bored any more. We have all sorts of projects. My favorite is reading and playing games with children in the hospital. I like it so much I'm thinking of becoming either a nurse or a social worker."

A final word about boredom: if you are bored you are also boring. Boredom makes the prettiest face sullen and unpleasant. The most striking characteristic in women who find love and happiness is a sparkling, outgoing zest for life.

Another top troublemaker is Jealousy, which usually takes the form of an "I'll show 'em" attitude. Melinda is invited to a big university hop; you're home watching TV. Barbara is going to Europe for the summer; you'll be at the lake. Other girls are doing this, that and the other, being fussed over, admired, pushed into the limelight; your life is a bleak gray.

What About Teen-Age Marriage?

What would get you talked about, make you the center of attention, have your phone clanging night and day? Getting married of course! You and your steady have talked it over, so why not? You and your friends have drooled over the fabulous wedding gowns in the bridal shops, mentally trying them on. You've thumbed through the bridal magazines and sighed through the newsreels of fairy tale weddings like Princess Margaret's. You wonder how it would feel if you were the bride moving slowly down the aisle, radiant in white, hundreds of friends and relatives watching you, their eyes brimming with happiness—and just that tiny trace of envy.

Wouldn't it be marvelous? Like starring in a Broadway play. But unlike a theatrical production, when you take your finery off you can't go home and pick up life where you left off. You are now a wife and when the tumultuous shouting dies and the guests depart, you may find yourself costarring in a drama which could turn into a tragedy.

Shakespeare called Jealousy the green-eyed monster. I'm not sure about the eyes but the monster description is true enough, a monster eating away at reason and sense. In one case, two sisters, Susan, sixteen, and Kathy, nineteen, spent their lives competing against each other. When Kathy made a new dressing table cover, Susan sat up all night making curtains and a bedspread. When Susan had her hair cut short, Kathy nearly went crew cut to "outshort" her. When Kathy announced her engagement, Susan told her best friend, "She thinks she's getting married first! Well, I'm going to beat her to it." Sure enough, a few weeks later, Susan eloped with a nineteen-year-old boy who at one time had been Kathy's steady. She beat her older sister to the altar, but she also beat her to a divorce. Within a year, Susan was back home, more miserable than ever, ashamed to face her friends at school, bitterly jealous of Kathy's happy marriage.

An old German proverb tells us "Jealousy does more harm than witchcraft." The best way to fight jealousy is to admit it; not to the world, just to yourself. If you feel overcome with rage or annoyance at somebody else, try to figure out, calmly and quietly, why.

"It's unfair!" you cry, pitying yourself because someone else has a better deal. You have just as good a figure as Beth's but she got a summer job modeling while you slaved as a waitress at a resort. You resent Beth's good fortune, avoid seeing her because you can't stand to hear about it. Months later you learn that the department store asked her to recommend another girl to model with her on Saturday afternoons and she was going to suggest you but thought you didn't want to be friends with her any more.

Perhaps another time your mother takes you shopping for a formal. You try on every dress in town but can't find the "right one." In the meantime, your mother picks up some things for your younger sister. "She gets everything! I get nothing!" you whine, forgetting the many times your mother has returned from a shopping trip with surprises for you.

Suppose success seems to come easily to some people and harder to you. Suppose some girls are naturally popular and you have to work at it. Suppose others are prettier, richer or more talented than you. Unfair?

Maybe it *is* unfair! The point is that life makes no guarantees. There's nothing in the Bible or anywhere else that says you *must* live happily ever after. You have to accept the fact that there will always be unfairness and try to remember the times when all the fairness was on your side. Don't let jealousy blind you to the ambitions and goals that can make you happy. Don't let jealousy plunge you into an "I'll show 'em" action that you'll regret.

The worst thing about jealousy is that it never does you any good. Crying your eyes out only gives you puffy eyes. Forcing a quarrel only gives you an enemy. Rushing into marriage for the sake of proving your own worth only gives you—and your husband—the enormous task of building a successful life on a rocky foundation.

Once you've faced your jealousy and figured out what's eating you, you'll find it won't bother you half so much. Sure, there are girls prettier, smarter, richer and luckier than you. Also sure, you are prettier, smarter, richer and luckier than thousands of others. So where does that leave you? Squarely on your own two feet with everything life has to offer waiting to be chased, fought for, worked for—and that includes marriage. But don't expect marriage to be The Answer to resentment, or you may then find yourself envious of those who've stayed single a while longer.

Having lunch in a drugstore one day I heard the pert coed beside me whisper to her girl friend, "Sometimes I feel so lonely, I could die!" Looking into the mirror across the counter I could see her blink back the tears. "Oh, cut it out," her friend said. "Have a malt. You'll feel better."

"Who needs a malt," she murmured in despair. "I know what I'm going to do. I'm going to get married!"

"Misery loves company," says the old English proverb, and you may meet a boy who is suffering from the same agonizing despair. You recognize each other as kindred spirits. You talk about your loneliness and your feelings of isolation from your family, from your classmates, from your friends. Perhaps you can help each other. Perhaps. Very likely, in fact. But is suffering together a basis for marriage? According to Dr. Marion Hilliard, many people marry because the loneliness of the other person is as urgent as their own. Being needed and needing are not enough, however, because a vacuum will still remain. On the other hand, feeling complete with someone is a very important part of love.

Two together *can* be as lonely as one. Think of the times you've been out with a boy and then found you had nothing to talk about, that the time dragged along and all you wanted to do was escape—go home. Translate this situation into two lonely people made even more lonely by rushing into a marriage which they hope will give them something they can only give themselves.

One of the maddening things about loneliness is that you suffer terribly but you don't look it. Nobody can guess at your anguish. Unless you confide in close friends or some close member of your family about it, how can they help you?

Actually, loneliness is part boredom, part uncertainty. This may sound like a sermon but loneliness boils down to having "nothing to do." Think of the people you know who always have too much to do. Life is too short for them. The days aren't long enough. Weekends zip by. They're always in a rush to get somewhere. They don't want to just hang around. And why are they never lonely?

Active interests. Purely and simply. If you have a tendency to feel lonely, steer clear of lone pursuits for the time being. Reading for hours, long walks and such are best saved for the time when you are content with yourself.

In the meantime, explore your potential talents, your craziest ambitions. If a boy you know helps you out of your loneliness, enjoy his company and share part of your life with him. Build a friendship. Help it grow. Make it a close, warm relationship. You'll find that once you connect with one person, you yourself will become more relaxed, better able to make richer and more worthwhile friendships.

A warm, close friendship, I repeat is the most important factor in love, so give it a chance to ripen. After you've learned the technique of developing friendships, you'll suddenly realize you can't marry every boy whose friendship means something to you.

Of more serious concern is a constant sense of aloneness. If you honestly feel as if you live in a vacuum, that you can't communicate, that months go by and you reach out for people but can't seem to touch them, then you must get help. Speak to your parents and tell them frankly how you feel. Or discuss it with your teacher, pastor, the family doctor or some older person you respect. Abject desolation can often be the result of some diet deficiency or some other physical or emotional problem.

Nobody watching you can ever tell whether or not you're suffering, whether or not your "moodiness" or "sulkiness" is superficial or whether you're really in need of help.

The mother of a high school senior told me, "In our family we respect each other's privacy, so that's why it was weeks before I realized Debbie spent too much time by herself in her room. One night after dinner I knocked on the door, and when she didn't answer I went in anyway. She was lying across her bed, dead asleep from exhaustion after an obvious crying jag. Her eyes were red and swollen and she was sobbing in her sleep. Later that night we had a long talk. At first she didn't want to admit anything was wrong but then she told me how lonely she was, that she didn't feel important to her father or me or any of her friends. She liked some of the boys she knew but didn't want to go steady or be engaged. She said she wished she could disappear into the ground."

Debbie's new-found closeness with her mother led her into making some discoveries about herself. She was "out of touch" with most people because she had placed herself out of touch, erecting a barrier around herself as if to say, "I'm here. If they want me, let them break through the barrier."

But they won't. The girl who sits by herself in the corner of the cafeteria, thinking, If they want me to eat with them, they'll find me and ask me, is in for a sad, lonely lunch. With the crowds and noise, nobody will notice, or if anyone does they'll think she wants to be alone to study or think.

If you feel lonely, out of reach, don't keep it to yourself. After all, you could be having an appendicitis attack, too, but unless you wail like a banshee how can anyone know by just looking at you?

Boredom, jealousy and loneliness are nothing compared to the biggest troublemaker of all—that horrible four-letter word—FEAR. You may "go steady" with somebody you're really not mad about because you're afraid to go to parties and dances alone, afraid of being a wallflower, afraid that nobody will ask you to dance or take you home.

When your friends begin to marry, you may suddenly panic because the marriage market, you feel, is getting smaller. All the good ones are being grabbed up. You may be left out.

As graduation approaches, you may realize all at once that you will soon be on your own, an adult expected to make your own living, settle into an adult social pattern. Going steady after graduation is possible but not very practical. The school functions you attended are finished for you. Homework is no longer a problem. Both of you are working. Are you afraid of meeting new men, afraid to have them ask you out on a date as an adult and not as a schoolgirl, afraid you can't handle passes, say Yes or No, make your own decisions?

Fear is not only uncomfortable, it robs you of experience, of gratification, of the thrill that comes with being an individual. You may be afraid of leaving home and sharing an apartment with other girls because you'll have to stand on your own two feet and cannot depend on your family to back you up.

You may be afraid of your growing sexual desires. You may worry that the pressures of sex will lead into trouble before you marry, that you may be unable to resist temptation, that something terrible may happen, such as pregnancy. You may feel that a quick marriage is the safe answer to all these fears.

As nineteen-year-old Dorothy explained bitterly, "I

was so afraid! It was the summer of my sixteenth birthday and it seems to me I was scared stiff of everything, mainly boys. I didn't have a steady but I found lots of boys sexy—and that worried me. To be honest, all I could think of was sex and there were three boys who were after me to go driving with them. I was afraid to go with any of them, scared silly I'd be carried away. At the end of the summer, one of the three boys, Billy, drove me home from a barbecue. We parked in the woods on the way. I was so overemotional, he asked me to marry him. We ran away the next weekend but we only stayed married a year."

Becoming an old maid may worry you, too, especially if you know some unmarried older women of twenty-eight or thirty who have dull lives. The thought of the same fate gives you goose pimples, haunts you with the specter of being left alone and loveless.

Agnes was unnerved by a talk she had with an unmarried cousin who visited her family for a weekend. Julia was twenty-nine, had a nice apartment and a good job. Peevishly calling herself a dried-up spinster, she had urged, "Get a husband any way you can, while the getting is good. Any husband is better than no husband. Living alone is awful."

What Julia didn't know is that if you let fears get the best of you while you're single, they're not going to disappear just because you get married. They'll just become different fears. Fear that your husband will stop loving you, fear that other women may try to take him away, fear of your in-laws. Once you let fear take over, you'll never be free of it.

A young wife seeking marital guidance said, "I thought marriage would cure my fears but it's only given them a new direction. Now I worry about whether my husband is going to like what I cooked for dinner. Sometimes, if he's ten minutes late coming home I'm practically hysterical. He tries to reassure me but I'm always afraid of losing him, afraid his boss will hate me, or his mother will tell him I'm not good enough for him."

Fear has no valid place in marriage. Fear doesn't build; it only destroys. If you are haunted by fears, try to recognize them for what they are and build up your resistance. If fear is warping your judgment, if you feel it is driving you to decisions such as marriage as a refuge, you must seek help from a premarital counselor or your clergyman. They will help you to find the reasons for these fears and to overcome them.

Don't get married because you are bored or jealous or lonely or afraid. Don't just sit there, of course. Do something constructive and enjoyable. Do develop your personality and skills. Do get married because you are genuinely in love, because you are a capable adult, because you feel able to take on and savor fully the responsibilities and rewards of family life.

3

THE REBEL

James Dean was a rebel. A restless, passionate creature, he defied convention, broke all the rules, lived by a law entirely his own. He thumbed his nose at fate and at a very early age wound up dead.

Jacqueline Bouvier was also a rebel. A restless creature, she defied her family's plans for her to be a debutante, studied photography and got a job as a photographer on a Washington, D.C., newspaper. On assignment she met Senator John F. Kennedy and wound up as First Lady of the land.

Both were rebellious young people, talented and ambitious. The difference? Jimmy Dean's rebellion was *de*structive. He risked the lives of other people as well as his own by tearing along a busy highway at over a hundred miles an hour. Jackie Kennedy's rebellion was *con*structive. She turned down the kind of life planned for her but buckled down to learning the skill that was to bring her romance, marriage and a place in history.

These are two extremes, of course, yet they point up the fact that being a rebel in the negative sense—that is, without a cause—may be exciting in the abstract but gets you nowhere fast. In contrast, a rebel *with* a cause, who refuses to accept things as they are, can have a rich, exciting life. Refusing to conform does not mean kicking over all the traces, turning your back on all decency and convention. Some of the most successful people were—and are—rebels who know precisely what they want, work for it in their own particular way, take chances and achieve their goals—whether it is in becoming a movie star, working their way around the world, or building their own boat in the back yard.

The "I'll show 'em" rebel cuts off her nose to spite her face. Sure they'll be sorry if you die, but you'll be even sorrier. Sure you can run away from home. Hero-

ines are always running away but they have authors
to look after them, to see to it that the heroes find them
and take care of them, whereas you may wind up in a
railway station with no money or food and an even
chance of being picked up by the police. Leaving home
is a good thing at the right time. When you're ready
to go, do so with some dignity and some preparation.
Have some money and a place to stay wherever it is
you're going. Be prepared for a certain amount of loneliness while getting settled with a job and meeting new
friends.

A wild sex life is another form of rebellion that
doesn't pay. You may be getting even with someone
you feel has done you wrong—perhaps your family or
a boy who won't pay any attention to you. But it's spit-
ing yourself again because you, not "they," get the bad
reputation. You suffer from the loss of boys' respect
once the word gets around that you're a pushover. You
hate yourself because of the merry-go-round you can't
jump off and the constant threat of pregnancy.

Eloping is another rebellion that is very romantic in
theory. Secrets and surprises are always thrilling. But
in some ways an elopement is like tinting your hair a
startling shade. You're dying to see how it will look.
What will everyone say? Did they think you'd have the
nerve? Wait till you see their faces! Well, when you do
it you might look in the mirror and faint! Or you might
decide it isn't that revolting and keep wearing it that

way for a time. Or you might think it's a change, all right, but not exactly what you want.

With an elopement, too much is at stake for a mis- ✗ take, and the pleasure of "showing" people won't make up for the unhappiness.

Instead of just saying "Cut it out!" and letting it go at that, I think that here is a good place to discuss the real reasons you feel rebellious, why you feel double-crossed and what makes you bitterly determined to pay back the sometimes real, sometimes imagined, failures of those around you.

A frequent complaint is "They don't care so I don't care." One girl whose mother thoughtlessly said she didn't care what she wore to a family party, came in dirty jeans, a torn sweater and false eyelashes. She shocked the family but she also scared the life out of a boy whom a cousin had brought along especially to meet her.

There's no getting around it. You may suffer from an acutely sensitive feeling of rejection as a teen-age girl and, realizing this, you must guard against feeling slighted when nothing of the kind is intended. You don't get invited to a certain party. A friend of yours doesn't see you on the street. Your teacher doesn't compliment you on a particularly good essay. Your parents buy something for one of the other children. You may magnify these oversights until the chip on your shoulder weighs a ton.

And then what? Then, unfortunately, it gets worse.

The more you brood about people "doing you wrong," the more they seem to do it. It's easy to come to the wrong conclusions and often you are wrong. A boy doesn't telephone the night he said he would—and next day he calls to say his mother was sick. Your family seems totally unaware of your birthday until the surprise party after dinner. Your English teacher has ignored your obvious interest in dramatics—and then hands you one of the leads in the class play.

To be wanted, you have to want. To be cared for, you have to care. But more than secret wanting and caring, you have to participate. Sitting in a corner and thinking, If they want me to help decorate the gym, they'll ask me, will probably find you still sitting in the corner when the gym is ready. Instead, you should go to the gym and offer your services.

Show others that you want them. Instead of waiting for someone in the lunchroom to ask you to sit with them, ask them to sit with you. Ask your father to go for a walk or a drive. Tell your mother you'd like to have a private talk with her. The difference between wanting and getting is knowing how to give and how to accept.

Another species of Rebel is the Maverick, the Loner. After running with the herd all your life, you suddenly want to cut loose, break away completely. Aside from being a television show, a maverick is in essence a runaway steer who shoots off blindly in any open direction and has to be rescued before he gets lost or dies of starvation. A maverick isn't particularly interested in "getting even" or "showing" anybody.

Pranks, practical jokes, crazy parties, impossible ambitions are made for mavericks. A runaway marriage in a borrowed car is great fun, but suddenly the joke is on you.

A nineteen-year-old divorced mother told me, "We ran away and got married Bill's graduation day. I still had a year to go but it didn't matter. It was June and moon and all that—and it seemed like such a great idea so we did it. By the end of the summer we were ready to forget the whole thing, but then I was pregnant and so we decided to make a go of it. Of course I couldn't go back to school—and about a year later we were fighting so much and were so unhappy that I moved back home with my folks. But now I feel too old to finish high school and the boys act kind of peculiar because I've already been married—and I don't know what to do. It's crazy but I feel like my life is over—at nineteen."

One of today's best-known alibis for almost every conceivable mistake is that Big Excuse known as The Unhappy Childhood. A thief says he steals because his mother was unkind to him. A murderer says his father hit him. A prostitute moans she wants only the love she was denied as a child.

Undoubtedly Adolf Hitler had an unhappy childhood, too, and the parallel can go on and on.

If yours was a home broken by death or divorce or

circumstances, if you never knew the solid sense of belonging to a closely knit, affectionate family, then you know to some degree what you have missed, and what you want to attain for yourself and your children.

To recognize what you have missed is one thing. To blame all your failures and defeats on it is not only unrealistic but can only make you a thoroughly miserable adult. Thomas Wolfe said, "You can't go home again." You can't change the past. You shouldn't allow the past to ruin your future.

These "Broken Home Blues" are a sad and plaintive wail. When parents are separated by divorce, or illness, or one of them dies, of course you will suffer. But instead of wallowing in your misery, learn from it. If you've ever been rescued from drowning, pulled through a deathly sickness or been saved from a fire, you know how deliriously wonderful it is to be alive.

If you've survived childhood, however rough it may have been, you've won a victory. You may feel slightly scarred but you've passed your preliminary tests and now you're ready for the main event.

Looking back in anger or helpless regret can only give you a stiff neck. When you've known what a broken home is and how it can affect children, you must think carefully and clearly before setting up your own home.

As for escaping from a broken home, by all means escape! Finish school. Plan your future. Earn some money. Leave home in an orderly manner and take a job rather than a husband as your first step to independence. You can always change jobs; you can't change husbands that easily.

On the other hand, if you've been suffocated by an overly loving family, watched over, protected until you feel if you don't make one decision for yourself you'll scream, be careful how you cut those apron strings.

There is no such thing as complete freedom, unless you want to live without love. Love means an interdependence, a giving and taking. It isn't necessary to run away from home or get married if your sole object is escape. Cut the apron strings, yes! Take some pretty strong measures, if necessary. But don't slash at those apron strings with your eyes tightly shut. Untie them calmly and neatly.

It's amazing how a little self-assertion works.

A well-dressed sixteen-year-old told me, "My mother never let me pick out any of my own clothes. She always tried to put me in baby dresses. We were always fighting at the store. It was very embarrassing. She looked me over every time I left the house to see whether maybe I might look too old for my age. There was a big fight every day. Then, last Christmas, I worked as a waitress over the holidays. I saved forty-five dollars and then I told Mother straight out I was going to spend it on the clothes that I wanted, not that she wanted. Funny thing is, she said okay and that it was my money and I could do what I wanted with it. Then, for no reason, she kissed me!"

Parents aren't perfect. Often they are overly protective because they want you to grow up healthy and strong. They tend to nag: "Eat more of this! Drink more of that! Take care of this! Do that!" Nagging becomes a habit until they're not even aware of it. But you are—and often you defend yourself by pleading, "Stop nagging me!" in an exasperated whine.

You can't fight nagging with more nagging. Instead, wait until your annoyance has calmed down, and then ask your mother or father (or both) to please sit down quietly because something is bothering you. Ask them not to interrupt until you've finished saying your piece. If you think you'll forget what you want to say or perhaps get mixed up, write it out ahead of time as if preparing a speech. Memorize it if possible. Explain how hemmed in you feel, how you've thought of doing something crazy like running away or eloping, how much you enjoy your home and want to stay in it but how difficult it is when you're treated like a three-year-old instead of an adult.

Sarcasm and sniping will only ruin things. A calm discussion, with no rancor, can work miracles of new understanding and appreciation between you and your family.

"Who needs Algebra?" is a familiar Rebel Yell. Jobs are plentiful. Money's around. Why bother with school when some easy job can earn you enough money for all the clothes, make-up and records you need? Fair enough. It certainly is more fun to have plenty of spending money and no homework than to eke through on a paltry allowance and grind away every night.

But to rebel against education means turning your back on the richest of life's gifts and the most rewarding. That's why parents and teachers get so excited about education, why they want you to get as much as you can. Not for abstract reasons of poetry and thousand-year-old cultures. But for very practical purposes.

Education opens doors. Study agriculture and home economics and you can work on a scientific farm for the summer or sign up with a government project such as the Peace Corps, in the meantime learning about food and nutrition that will always come in handy when you're married. Work at a foreign language and you can then get a job as an interpreter or in an expensive shop dealing with overseas visitors or with a travel agency requiring bilingual personnel.

The attitude of "Here I am—take me or leave me" may find you stuck in a dull job with none of the experience or background to equip you for an interesting one. Even if you're planning to work only until you marry, don't waste your job experience on something dull. Find a job you can sink your teeth into. You've heard of bored young wives and straying husbands who are in turn bored with their wives because they have nothing to say. They say nothing because, sadly, they have nothing *to* say. Their eyes have not been opened. The magic of art or music or science or literature or history eludes them because their appetite has not been sparked. They have no idea what's going on, and soon they don't care. The dull rot sets in and they become automatons, barely able to understand the newspapers —if, in fact, they even bother to read them—because they don't know the places, the people, and have no idea what's happening here or in other countries.

Granted that some subjects are rough, math and science are generally considered the roughest. Rather than face failing them you may decide to forget the whole thing and go to work. An easier way in the long run is to determine to squeak through on the difficult subjects and concentrate your pleasure and devotion on the subjects you like. French. English. History. Take in as much as you can of the commercial skills. Typing. Steno. Bookkeeping. You'll need them as much to run an efficient home as an efficient office.

And if you've been dreaming of some pet project, don't be ashamed to go it alone. Maybe you're fascinated by archeology and the excavation of ancient ruins. Perhaps social work appeals to you with its responsibility toward less fortunate members of the community. Then there are catering, beauty culture, photography and countless other exciting fields that will make having a career an exciting challenge and add a great deal to your future marriage.

Being a rebel is a natural instinct of a young, healthy animal. Don't let the spirit of rebellion run away with you. Control it and make it work for you. Don't gorge the whole box of chocolates in one day. Spread the wealth out. Live for today—and tomorrow, too.

4

DANGERS OF ELOPEMENT

You've run away. Some friends came along to stand up for you and afterward you went to a roadside café and laughed and clowned around and drank a little too much to cover up that gnawing worry, "What have we done?"

The main point about runaway marriage is that the elopement itself is sleazy. Your choice of a husband may be the right one. It's your haphazard way of getting married that can spell T-R-O-U-B-L-E from the start. Not between the two of you, not right away. Because you're sure of your love and intoxicated with the adventure of an elopement. But being married means being part of the community, living in the warmth of their respect and affection.

Being objective, what's the first thing you think of when you hear about an elopement? The girl must be in trouble! It's an inevitable reaction, and when you return you find yourself the uneasy victim of eyes glued to your waistline, discreet finger-counting and persistent questioning about how soon you're going to have a baby.

Reputation is a precious thing. By running away you have in effect abandoned your friends and family, and when people's feelings are hurt they look for some sinister reason. Gossip may plague the first few months of your marriage until the know-it-alls are satisfied and you are in the position of having to put up with it in teeth-gritting silence. This is one situation where protesting too much sounds like guilt.

In addition, eloping sounds as if you haven't a deep enough respect for marriage. If you did you would go about it in the conventional way. By not conducting yourselves as responsible adults, you can't be too surprised when neighbors dismiss you as a couple of silly kids.

The kind of elopement under discussion is one in which you rush off, get married and return home, with no clear idea of where you're going to live—or how.

Occasionally, young couples are unhappy in their home town and run away to start a new life away from previous associations. They know they will face loneliness but feel that together they will have the strength to succeed.

With economic conditions as they are today, most young people want to stay in their own community, help it develop and grow, raise their children among familiar places and people. To live a respectable life in the community, you need the respect of the community.

Another—very personal—danger is that you and your husband may not feel "really married." Without a proper religious ceremony and the presence of those near and dear, you will be legally wed but you may miss the serious spiritual bond so necessary to a lasting marriage. A two-minute ceremony in some remote office may seem more and more like a make-believe stunt, like dressing up when you were children. You may secretly feel you're "living in sin" and discover it's not as romantic a feeling as you supposed.

On the very practical level there is the matter of wedding presents. Not only will you miss the good wishes of friends and family that give you confidence for your new venture, but you will miss most of the gifts traditionally bestowed on newlyweds. Wedding gifts are not merely part of a money-making scheme thought up by department stores. Wedding gifts are an essential to the start of every marriage. They are everyone's way of helping you get launched. In the days of pioneers, they had "barn-raising" parties for newlyweds, where the entire settlement worked together to build a barn in one day. Today's bride and groom get a toaster, cutlery, linen, lamps and almost all of the bits and pieces that make a house into a real home.

When you deny friends and relatives the joy of participating in your wedding, whether it's for the ceremony or a reception afterward, they feel unnecessary, unwanted and disinclined to make their contribution to a marriage from which they have been barred. Being married among kin and friends gets you off to a sound spiritual as well as material good start with the best wishes and support of everyone.

You may say you have each other so who needs anything more? If you're honest, you'll know that you will need all the help you can get.

Worst of all, the old cliché about hating yourself in the morning may suddenly and sadly apply, if not the first morning then very shortly afterward as reproaches begin and each of you blames the other for rushing into something too fast. You may each feel vaguely cheated, vaguely cheap in the eyes of the other. As mutual respect fades, so does mutual confidence.

While elopement may set the town on it's ear, make

you minor celebrities for a few days, after that, you may be left with a memory book containing a crushed corsage and a newspaper clipping headed "Local Girl Elopes."

Well, then, if an out-and-out elopement is too risky and you feel you can't possibly wait half a second longer to be married, what about a Secret Marriage? The delicious idea of belonging completely to one another, no holds barred, with nobody knowing and the whole thing legal is very romantic. Also, you're in the clear if you become pregnant because, after all, you *are* married, aren't you?

Legally, yes, but being married is not just having an intimate sexual relationship. Marriage is living together, adjusting your habits, tastes and idiosyncrasies to the habits, tastes and idiosyncrasies of the other.

Secret marriages are a cheat, in several ways. First of all, the delight of sex is a continuing reward in your early days of married life when the dinner burns and the tub overflows and you forget to pick up the laundry. This intimacy binds you closely together while all kinds of unnerving things try to yank you apart.

If you dissipate all the joys of sexual happiness in a secret marriage before you have a home together, you'll be unprepared and ill-equipped later on. Like the child whose mother put chocolate syrup in her milk because she hated milk. One day the child ate all the chocolate syrup first and then had to drink the milk plain. The

61

sweet and not-so-sweet taste better when mixed together.

When a baby is on the way, you face the emotional avalanche of telling everyone you're already married. Not being at your best physical peak in the first months of pregnancy, you'll have all the difficulty of finding a proper place for you and your husband to live while at the same time you'll be going to the doctor and taking care of yourself in preparation for childbirth.

As the reality of pregnancy dawns on you, you and your young husband may begin to feel extremely young and trapped by the coming baby. You've loved each other in the deepest physical sense, but you've had no actual experience or preparation for living together as a married couple. As happens in many secret marriages, you may never have spent a whole night together in bed and now, suddenly, you're expected to be an old married couple, with a baby on the way, while as far as actual marriage is concerned, you haven't even had a honeymoon.

In recent years, there have been epidemics of secret marriages in many parts of the country. Nobody knows how they start, but all at once "everybody's doing it." In Tucson, Arizona, twenty girls at one high school married secretly within four months, a statistic which only gradually came out because of pregnancy or other reasons. In Texas and Oklahoma, Elopement Fever swept the schools, including nine cases in which the bride was still in elementary school. In Charlotte, North

Carolina, a few years ago, the marriage bug hit one high school—with nearly four per cent of the student body getting married.

How did most of them work out? Though it would be unfair to condemn them all, it is only fair to observe that the success stories are the exception and concern exceptional young people. George, at sixteen, was editor of the school paper, top male scholar and voted "most likely to succeed" when he and Rita, also a good student, confessed they had been married for several months. Rita became pregnant, quit school. George worked Saturdays, maintained his high scholastic level until high school graduation. George is working full time now and going to college at night. Not yet twenty, George and Rita have two children and are superbly happy. On their side has been an enormous capacity for work, tremendous physical energy and intellectual drive.

Unhappily, most secret marriages do not fare so well. "We had stars in our eyes," said Carole miserably, married at fourteen, a mother at fifteen, divorced at sixteen. "Sure I knew I was young but plenty of other girls were doing it—and besides, it was all so easy."

Karen and Tom, fifteen and sixteen, drove across the state border after a school dance and had regrets before completing the homeward journey. They don't "feel married" and haven't decided how to face the future.

Joanna, not quite eighteen now, eloped at sixteen and was a divorced mother at seventeen. She says soberly, "I don't want to marry again just to give my baby a father. This time I'll have to be in love and want to marry because he'll make both a good husband and a father."

To my mind, May and June are the danger months for rash elopements. Nature is awakening and so are you. Winter wools have been replaced by bareback cottons, stockingless legs. The nights are unbearably romantic with the intoxicating smell of grass and flowers. There is sweet-sad poignancy in spring dances, the end of school term, possibly graduation.

The good times are now—and suddenly you don't want to let them go. You're young. You're in love. The world is made for lovers. If you don't make a grab for happiness now, you're convinced it may elude your grasp forever.

Love often ripens in the spring, as do the fruit and the flowers. If it does, nurture it tenderly. Give it time to flower. If you pluck it too soon, it may wither and die. If you push it too far, it may die on the vine.

Allow love to flourish fully. It is a delicate bud and requires care.

There is an old country proverb about knowing your loved one through the changes of four seasons before marrying. It's a good thing to remember.

But if you've breathlessly decided on an elopement, before you slide down that knotted sheet, ask yourself these questions:

1. Has your school work been slipping so badly that you're afraid to face failure?

An elopement would certainly take everybody's mind off your marks.

2. Is your boy friend going into the service or away to college and you feel you can't face the separation?

An elopement can only compound the complications.

3. Were you madly in love and frantic to get married to someone else a short time ago?

Then you are in love with the idea of love, and an elopement would only mean a romantic escapade.

4. Will you feel the same about your boy friend in six months?

If you don't feel confident enough to wait and see, an elopement is pretty sad insurance for lasting love and happiness.

If all of this sounds pretty "anti-elopement," that's exactly what it's meant to be, and for the very reasons given. Not because "It's not nice" or "You don't know what you're doing." You do know what you're doing. You're making a bid for happiness but you handicap your chances.

The ingredients may be right but the timing is wrong. Take a cake out of the oven before it's ready and it will collapse. Take the rollers out of your hair before it dries and it, too, will fall apart. Marriage requires preparation, patience and a sure knowledge of what you're doing.

Your choice of a husband may be the right one, and the marriage essentially a good idea for this reason. But an elopement may start it off too soon and on the wrong foot. It may never stop limping.

5

IF HE'S OLD ENOUGH FOR THE SERVICE, WHY NOT MARRIAGE?

Two years is an awfully long time. More than that, it's an eternity. You're afraid that while *he's* away he'll find new interests, new people and forget all about *you*. He's afraid that while he's away *you'll* find new interests, new people and forget all about *him*. You love each other dearly. You know it would be more practical to wait but you don't want to risk the chance of losing each other, so what can you do?

Everyone says you're too young. You reason that if he's old enough to leave home and serve in the armed forces for two years, he's mature enough for marriage, and that goes for you, too.

So you decide to get married.

What happens then?

Will it work? Can it work? What are the pitfalls?

Like the song says, it all depends on you.

A twenty-year-old husband told me, "We're settled down at home now but we wouldn't have given up those two years I was in the Army for anything. Claire was a camp follower for the first year. Then she went home to have the baby and then they both spent the last six months in town near my base. When I had a pass, we were squashed in one room but it was worth it. Now we have a four-room apartment and it's like heaven. We feel our marriage is on a solid foundation and it might not have worked out if we'd waited."

On the other hand, a girl who ruefully described herself as a GI divorcée said, "I couldn't stand staying in a poky little hotel room for days on end with nothing to do and nobody to talk to, waiting for Bob to get a few hours off. So we decided that was no good for either of us because we spent the little time we did have together fighting instead of loving. But being home with my folks was worse. I was an army widow. I couldn't go out at night because I was married and people might talk. All of my friends were talking about their boy friends and all I had to show were Bob's letters. After a few months, I got so desperate I started going out anyway. Then I fell in love with somebody else. By the time Bob got discharged, I knew I didn't love either of them. We got a divorce and now I'm plain scared of marriage."

If you are the Wife Who Goes Along, you shoulder an enormous responsibility that your husband can't help with because his actions are heavily restricted by duty. You must make your own travel arrangements, and when you get to the town nearest the training camp you have to find your own place to live, in a small hotel or rooming house. You may be able to find a job to pass the time and earn some money but with so many service wives in the area, this may not be possible.

To live on a husband's salary and allotment may mean having to cook on a tiny stove or eating in cheap restaurants, doing all your own laundry, and fighting boredom. You may sometimes have to wait two or three weeks at a time to see your husband and then he may be so exhausted that all he wants to do is sleep while you want to go out on the town because you haven't stirred for days.

You may feel the kind of loneliness you never thought possible. You're cut off from home, from family and friends and also from your husband's life which has become a lot of unintelligible gibberish about his training

—sprinkled with slang which he knows you can't understand but which he's proud of just the same.

The Wife Who Stays Behind has other problems. There is the loneliness of two years of "widowhood" as described by the young divorcée. You may say that by marrying you'll have emotional security, someone to hold onto, if only in your dreams. But is it security? If you're left behind, you have a ring on your finger and the love light in your heart, but you're living in a social and emotional vacuum. However much you love him, you'll find it rough hanging suspended for two years, neither wife nor bachelor girl, living on letters, phone calls and an occasional few days together.

While he's expanding his horizons, experiencing a new way of life, you are prohibited from enjoying your old life as a single girl, and your new life as a young married woman without her husband is quite limited. You may worry that you are getting duller day by day because there's nothing to stimulate your interest. You can go out to dances and parties in groups, of course, but then there's the problem of getting you home. If one man takes you home, there's gossip. If you receive a group escort all the time, you become a burden on your friends.

True, living at home with your family and having a job can fill your time quite well. You can save money, write your husband every day, go to bargain sales and auctions to choose furnishings for your future home at your leisure.

Face the fact that until he comes home, you will be both a wife without a husband and a teen-ager without the right to act like one.

The situation changes if you have a baby. Once again, the total responsibility will be yours. You may even have to give birth with your husband hundreds of miles away. Of course family and friends will rally around but your husband won't be there to share the first months of the baby's life. These are experiences you should have together. Your letters can't re-create reality.

When he returns to a ready-made family, he may be rarin' to go as a honeymooner, whereas you are up to your ears in baby's bottles, diapers, teething—and which shoulder gives the better burp.

Although he will certainly adore the baby, it will be more of a cute toy or puppy dog to him because he hasn't gone through the initial growing pains with you.

Whether you stay home or camp-follow, there are other considerations. First of all, your schooling. You may quit before graduation, feeling that school is a waste of time, but it isn't a waste of time, particularly if you plan to go to work. Without that high school diploma, your wage level is rock bottom. Many companies won't take you except for the most menial jobs. Their attitude is that if you don't think enough of your own intelligence to finish high school, you won't think enough of a job to have a responsible attitude.

Your earning power until the arrival of babies keeps

you home is an immediate concern. But looking ahead, as a wife with a poor education you can never quite hold up your head. You'll always feel slightly inferior to others, and when the children begin to grow up you'll feel ashamed of your ignorance, of being unable to help them with their homework, unable to face them squarely when they ask about your schooling, unable to command respect when advising them.

Meanwhile your husband's two years in service are developing his mind and his skills. He's learning things he never thought of before. He will probably go on loving you but he may secretly think of you as a cute little dope and conclude you're not quite bright enough to discuss with him his innermost thoughts and ambitions.

Lack of education is a kind of prison. It cuts you off from earning power and intellectual respect, depriving you of the tools of thinking, reading and searching that make life exciting.

Readjusting to civilian life after two years of service is difficult for your husband and can be hard on you. He may have made new friends, adopted new habits. He may feel slightly bewildered and edgy to be his own master again after months of obeying orders.

You may find after a long separation that you've become strangers, pen pals who write letters to each other rather than husband and wife, and you may find it hard to get to know each other again. Whereas you were students when you married, you're not any longer and the adult world is highly competitive.

Should you decide not to marry just yet but to wait until he comes home, you will feel more closely tied if you become formally engaged before he leaves. This will give each of you official status in terms of your future marriage. It will permit you to visit him during his training. It will give you both the security of a troth plighted without the overwhelming responsibility of a marriage you are not free to enjoy fully.

You can continue your schooling, if desired, save money, enjoy the social life of an engaged girl, limited according to your own wishes. He can concentrate on his training, safe in the knowledge that you're waiting for him.

You'll miss each other terribly, but so would you if you were married. You'll each be able to go out on casual dates without feeling unfaithful, because an engagement is a matter of trust that is all the more binding since it can be broken at any time.

And should the worst happen, should you fall in love with someone else or he with another girl, remember that the risks are the same when you're separated a long time, whether you're married or not.

Think of what you were like two years ago. Try to imagine what you may be like two years hence. You'll be different and so will he. You will not have had the chance to do your growing up together.

The love that survives a two-year separation is a strong, true love and will surely culminate in a richly satisfying marriage.

6

TALKING THINGS OVER

There is the traditional image of the mother who cuts off her children's questions by urging, "Eat first, talk later! The food will get cold." If you're considering marriage, your actions should be quite the reverse. Talk first, let the idea of marriage cool down to room temperature while you find out whether or not it's your dish.

Talking out a situation is the best way to clarify it. Talk as much and with as many people as you think will shed some light on the subject. Questions, doubts and confusions tend to sort themselves out when aired. Most likely you've discovered this fact for yourself, like the time you "didn't know what to do" about a family situation and a heart-to-heart discussion with your best friend suddenly made the solution crystal clear.

First and foremost, do you really and truly want to get married now? Or do you simply want to leave home? Does your family's disapproval of your boy friend upset you, drive you to his defense? Are you wondering whether you are too young to marry? Have you doubts about finance, questions about sex, worries about having babies?

Go to people you trust and respect. Ask their advice, make use of their experience. Talk to an older married couple whose married life you admire, a favorite teacher who always talks straight from the shoulder, a minister or social worker concerning the deeply perplexing problems of religious or moral conviction. There should be no holds barred in these conversations. What you don't say before marriage may be the cause of unspeakable misery afterward.

Give your parents a chance to be helpful. Often they may be too closely involved to give unemotional and objective opinions but you can be certain they will talk from the heart. Though the expression "for your own good" may make you cringe, certainly of all the people in your life, your parents want to see you happily married. Admittedly, parents are sometimes unwilling or unable to break through the barrier they have erected between themselves and their children. But be fair with them, give them a chance to reach you.

"My mother was always very strict," recalls an eighteen-year-old bride. "I was very unhappy at home. Then, one day, when I was fifteen, I fell in love with a man of twenty-three. We wanted to get married. My mother yelled at me, said I didn't know what I was doing. I yelled back, said I couldn't stand living with her another minute. So then she cried and told me all about what happened when she was a teen-ager, how she eloped with a boy from the next town and how sorry she was almost the same minute, and how their fathers had the marriage annulled. She told me she was strict because she didn't want me to get into trouble or do something I'd regret. Then we talked for hours and I suddenly realized that I didn't really want to get married. I only wanted to be close to somebody."

As a result, she finished high school and at eighteen married someone entirely different.

Sex rears its fascinating head in all marriage discussions. One girl I met confided to me that she was sure there was something wrong with her insides but she was ashamed to go to a doctor because she wasn't married, afraid he might not examine her, or scold her for being wicked. "Ever since I first started getting my period, I've had terrible pains," she said. "And not only during it but other times, too. I'm afraid that the doctor will ask me if I pet. I have but I couldn't stand telling him about it." She didn't stop to think that doctors know all about sex and understand the problems of young people. The doctor's job is to help you. He has seen and heard everything. Nothing you can tell him will startle him, nor will he stand in judgment of your behavior.

Years ago, menstruation as well as other body functions were discussed in whispers of misinformation and scary "old wives' tales." Today, menstruation is candidly discussed in schools, books, magazine articles and in most homes. Yet even today a few of the old bugaboos persist and may cause unhappiness. If you hear anything at all about menstruation that worries you— however farfetched—immediately talk to your mother or hygiene teacher. Even if you only half believe something disturbing, ask about it so you won't be secretly and needlessly concerned.

You've doubtless heard about gynecologists and may perhaps have wondered what, exactly, a gynecologist is. A gynecologist is either a man or woman doctor who specializes in the care and treatment of the reproductive parts of the female. A gynecologist often delivers babies, although sometimes he will turn this responsibility over to an obstetrician who devotes his entire practice to obstetrics, or childbirth.

If you have any worries about your body, fears about your period or suspect any irregularity, ask your family doctor to recommend a gynecologist. If he tells you to stop being silly and wait until you're married, which is sometimes the advice of well-meaning but unfeeling doctors, then call your local office of the American Medical Association or the best maternity hospital in your area and ask for the name of a reputable gynecologist.

Will he see you if you're not married? Of course. He will see you, explain things about your body you may not know, and answer your questions. If you change your mind about being examined, you can leave. A doctor's office is not a prison.

You must, however, be honest with a doctor. A young friend of mine was walking around in a state of hysteria, moody, tearful, absolutely frantic. Finally, she broke down and admitted that she thought she was pregnant. She had missed a period. She was nauseated in the morning. All the symptoms she'd ever read about were there.

No, she confessed, she hadn't had the nerve to go to the doctor, so we went together. It turned out that she was not only not pregnant but was still a virgin. The "false pregnancy" was the result of a wild imagination and a deep sense of guilt. A few months earlier she had been more intimate in love-making than ever before and was so overwhelmed by guilt afterward that she couldn't remember exactly what had happened. She refused to see the boy again and was convinced she was pregnant and that it served her right for being bad. In a high state of tension she had examined her body every day, looking for signs of thickness. She woke up every morning expecting the dreaded sickness. She was so overwrought that soon her body created the very symptoms she most feared.

With the doctor's assurance and all these fears explained, she immediately felt fine and her body returned to its normal function.

If you are getting married, see the gynecologist with your husband-to-be. He may have some questions, too.

Five little words, "We're thinking of getting married," will give you the benefit of other peoples' experiences. Listen—and pick out the bits that will benefit you—and learn from those experiences.

Where certain definite problems exist, face them. If you're of different faiths, see a minister of both. Discuss whether one of you will change or each remain with your own beliefs, and how the decision will affect your children.

In matters of finance, especially, expert opinion is helpful. If either of you must contribute to the support of your parents or if there are debts or you both want to continue school and work, too, there are many social service agencies you can consult. Social workers and marriage counselors may be seen at your local civic welfare associations or found through universities, clinics and hospitals.

"I was just a 'crazy mixed up kid.' Instead of getting married, I should have seen a psychiatrist!" a bitter young mother of three explained. "I thought getting married would solve everything. What a laugh!"

Psychiatrists—"head doctors"—are the butt of many jokes, such as "You really have to be crazy to go to a psychiatrist." Yet psychiatry is neither a joke, a hobby nor some sort of mystical hocus-pocus. It is a science for helping people help themselves out of emotional disorders. Feeling insecure and unsure indicate typical teen-age emotions, but if you are convinced that everything you do is wrong, that all you can see ahead is darkness, that home, school, friends are all against you and that a golden marriage may be the one thing to save you, then it may be a good idea to seek professional help.

The human being is a functioning being, equipped to take care of its bodily needs, develop its mind, reason its course through life. If you are not functioning on all levels, if you feel bogged down in quicksand, again see your minister or your family doctor. Ask for advice in finding a suitable clinic or social agency where you can discuss your problems and see whether you need further therapy.

Rosemary was the middle sister in a family of three girls. Her older sister had married the president of the class, had two children and a big house. Her younger sister had won a scholarship. Rosemary entered a beauty contest but came in second. She was crazy about a boy on the debating team but since he didn't pay any attention to her she started to go steady with a boy who liked her, telling everyone they were going to elope until he, too, stopped seeing her.

All of a sudden, Rosemary's marks slipped way down; her appearance changed, she was messy, unattractive, her lipstick clashed if she wore lipstick at all. She became morose, eating lunch alone, "walking around like a zombie" as one of her friends said.

In effect, she had withdrawn from life. The family doctor had recommended a few sessions with a psychoanalyst. Soon, it became clear to her that she had decided not to compete any more because of a few initial defeats.

Everybody's always accusing teen-agers of talking too much. Pay no attention. Discuss. Listen. Learn.

7

HAPPILY EVER AFTER—
AND THEN WHAT?

Most love stories end at the altar. Organ music swelling. Mom whimpering into her corsage. Dad blinking bravely. Bride and groom triumphant under the benevolent eyes of the clergyman. Then come champagne, shoes, rice and, just when the Happily-Ever-After is about to begin—fade-out!

You've given your fans a lavish and dramatic production but when the audience goes home, there you are, all alone, with no stage manager to slip you your cue in case you forget your next move.

Wedding and marriage are clearly two separate words with two distinctly separate meanings. Being ready to wed means being ready for sex and procreation. A bit frightening, maybe, but relatively easy because sexual relations and childbearing are "doing what comes naturally," and your instincts will provide many of the answers to questions you haven't even thought of yet. Being ready for marriage, however, is something else and distinctly more demanding on your patience, ingenuity and maturity.

As a young wife candidly admitted, "Finding out about sex and eventually having our baby were hard enough. But what nearly broke us up were fights over things like using the car and cleaning up the apartment. My husband said I was a slob and I said I didn't get married to be his maid. Luckily we managed to work things out though of course we still have fights."

After the honeymoon, the first few days of being home and saying hello to everybody as a "married couple," the "—AND THEN WHAT?" begins. As a teen-age couple, you will suddenly have to contend with innumerable social, sexual, personal, emotional and economic adjustments.

Socially, you will find your life completely changed.

While you may feel that you are the same two kids you were a few weeks before the wedding, you may find that your unmarried friends will feel slightly estranged from you. You are a married couple now and not one of the gang. Almost certainly you'll continue to be invited to parties and the gang will come over to your place, but every couple interviewed reported the same chasm between themselves and their old friends.

You've completed the break with teenhood. They haven't. Your interests are different. You're involved with curtains, the butcher bills, having the laundry done, cooking meals; they still have their mothers to do these things. You have rightfully and confidently explored the mysteries of sex; they have not—and the difference in the status of your sex lives further separates you. They may secretly resent your knowledge, yet be unwilling to ask you questions.

So you drift away from your old chums, but you find that the age gap that separates you from most of the other married couples makes friendship with them difficult.

A seventeen-year-old wife, still at high school, said wistfully, "My club won't let me eat lunch with them because I'm married. They call me a traitor."

Another problem is spending money. Whereas formerly a part of your allowance or the money you earned after school went for bowling, movies and dancing, you may find your married budget is heavy on cornflakes, soap powders, payments on the television—with little left for outside entertainment or inviting people over.

Your break with the past is complete if you have a baby the first year. Naturally your old pals will be thrilled about the baby. They'll come and see it, cluster around the carriage when you go walking along the street or in the park. But then they'll be off to their own interests which have nothing to do with babies.

"I never felt so lonely in my life as I did the first year after the baby was born," a mother of eighteen recalled. "The baby was too small to really play with. Al was at work the whole day. My girl friends were at school until three and then they would stop by and say hello but they never stayed. My next door neighbor had a little boy of three but she was always giving me advice as though she were my mother or something, and all I could think of was how nice it would be to go shopping with my girl friends—except what would I do with the baby?"

Your husband's social life may take some adjusting to, as well. He may belong to a bowling club or have a hobby like cars or hunting which may take him away from the house and leave you alone. To expect your husband to give up these outside interests after marriage would be foolish because then he would feel "trapped" and resent it, might even be sorry he ever gave up his freedom. You, on the other hand, might feel excluded from his activities and pick fights with him about neglecting you.

Unfortunately, one of the big differences between men and women in love is that women love exclusively and possessively and tend to be jealous of everything that may distract their husband's attention from them, whereas a man can love one woman deeply and sincerely yet have the ability to surrender himself completely to a job or a hobby or a cause.

Another young wife said disgustedly, "The only people we see now are other married couples. The men sit around together in one room, the women in another. I don't know what the men talk about but I'm sure it's more interesting than ours. Recipes. Diaper rash. Which brand of soap gives you the most suds. Sometimes I could scream! It's all they think about."

Sexually, despite the freedom of marriage, you may find certain problems. Married sex is more than actual intercourse. It is the art of physically living side by side, sleeping in the same room, understanding and accepting the differences in body structure as well as body functions between a man and a woman. Personal hygiene comes into it, too. And cleanliness is a prime factor.

One young couple after a miserable first year of marriage took their problem to a marriage counselor. Before their marriage, Amy had been warm, affectionate and passionately responsive to Bud's love-making. They had never gone beyond a certain point and Amy was a virgin on their wedding day. To the dismay and misery of both, Amy became almost frigid after the wedding. She loved Bud deeply and sincerely yet she could not bring herself to go all the way. Bud was patient, sweet and tried to be understanding, but when neither time nor patience seemed to help, they sought out a marriage counselor.

The expert explained that theirs was not an isolated case, that in fact it happened quite often to other couples who were just as bewildered as they.

"How could it be?" Amy wanted to know. "For weeks before we got married it was agony. I felt as if I would explode if I couldn't go all the way. But we decided to wait and do the right thing. During the honeymoon, we thought everything went wrong because we were overtired from all the preparations and everything, but month after month went by and nothing went right."

What Bud and Amy failed to realize is that lovemaking in bed is not one step beyond love-making in a car or on the back porch. It is a completely different sort of love-making. It is love sanctified by the marriage contract and approved by society. Your mind recognizes this fact but your body has been conditioned by your premarital life, at which time love-making was considered wrong. You're allowed to taste it but not to drink your fill. From the first moment you become aware of the opposite sex, parents, teachers, advisers instruct and warn you to say "No, no, no." You are taught, rightly, to control your physical desires, to keep your animal instincts in check so that you don't turn into an animal, to squash your passions until the right time to release them.

Then, when you marry, your body may have difficulty in adjusting itself to giving instead of holding back. If you have trained it to restraint, slowly and carefully you will have to untrain it to respond unselfconsciously to the physical destiny for which it is made.

This is one of the problems in marriage which afflicts the teen-age bride especially because of her inexperience. However, it must be stated flatly right here, that sexual intercourse before marriage is not the answer because of the cheapening effect it has on your relationship.

I wouldn't presume to give an intimate guide to married love-making, but one factor does become obvious to most young marrieds. The hours of necking, petting and fondling, with one eye on the clock and separation impending, provide a different atmosphere for love-making from that of the safety and comfort of a bedroom. Whereas before you marry, you're frantic with the need to be alone somewhere in a warm, quiet room where you can take your clothes off and love each other in peace, after you're married the environment changes. You may not neck or pet on the couch because you can always go to bed. You may find yourselves undressing before each other without any noticeable rise in your temperature. You may be in bed together with little inclination for sex and wonder why this is so, forgetting your courtship and the hours of kissing and caressing that formerly built your passions to the pitch of wanting to be in bed.

On the purely personal side are your day-to-day habits and attitudes. You may like coffee and toast for breakfast while your husband wants a four-course meal, and expects you to cook it. Your courtship days may have revolved around hamburgers and chili; now your husband expects you to shop for and cook interesting meals—and no TV dinners, either. You may take ten minutes to get ready to go out while your husband takes an hour, or vice versa, to the annoyance of whoever is kept waiting. You may leave the bathroom in a state of upheaval, an eccentricity your mother used to cope with.

You give up some things, gain others. You give up thinking in terms of "I;" instead, everything is "We." If he sickens at chicken and you balk at pork, serve lamb chops, pot a roast, make a stew—and occasionally, for kicks, get some pork chops for him, a bit of poultry for you, and have a picnic.

It means giving up your privacy, too. If you enjoyed a room of your own in your parents' home, complete authority over your mail, your earnings, record collection, pastimes, you may find it intrusive to share everything with your husband and he may find the same difficulty. Rather than hold grudges about these things, discuss them openly. You don't like your magazines riffled through before you read them. Your husband likes his desk in chaos, not straightened up. Though compromise may sound like defeat, it is often the only way to mutual victory.

On the credit side, you gain much from learning by give-and-take. Two heads are definitely better than one when it comes to decisions. Sharing the other's interests broadens your own knowledge. You may find working a hand drill is thrilling and wind up building a cabinet. He may discover a hidden talent for concocting spaghetti sauce better than anything in Italy.

Finally, the conditions under which you live have a big effect on your "happily ever after." If you live with one of your families, you undergo the severe problems of not having privacy, and you need privacy to relax completely and learn all about each other with no inhibitions. You may want to sleep all day Sunday or have something to eat at three in the morning or skip dinner entirely without having to make excuses or explanations to anyone. But the family has its rules and routines by which you have to abide.

Living with one of your families extends the feeling that you are still children because there are mother and father giving advice, and you wind up like two naughty children with the privilege of sleeping together but little else that constitutes a real marriage. With parents so close, they can't help expressing opinions and trying to settle disputes between you, which you should work out entirely by yourselves.

"We lived with Mary's family because they had a big house and we didn't have much money. But Mary kept on being a daughter instead of becoming a wife. She wanted to be married to me but she still didn't want to leave her folks' house because it was so comfortable and her mother fussed over us as if we were toys. I found us a furnished room with a kitchen and insisted we move in. Mary's mother was horrified. How could her daughter live like that? Mary came with me but after two months she was horrified too, and she went back home. I guess modern plumbing meant more to her than marriage. We're divorced now."

On the other hand, setting up housekeeping means suddenly switching from the comparatively simple management of your school allowance to the much more complex management of a household budget. This requires a trial-and-error frankness on the part of both. You might start out spending your money one way and find yourself swamped with debts because of mistaken calculations. You must be especially careful with installment buying. Don't saddle yourself with too many monthly payments. One unexpected emergency may find you in hock—and your half-paid-for TV, hi-fi and freezer being carted away because of lapsed payments.

Most likely your first home will be pretty makeshift. You'll have to adjust to shared discomfort, closets too small, not enough space for your belongings, problems of heat and light.

Will you "live happily ever after" and laugh about these early days? Perhaps the experiences of others will give you a clue to your own potential. Here are capsule opinions of sixteen teen-age brides interviewed in a study by Dr. Lee Burchinal, professor of sociology, Iowa State College. Eight are glad they married young, eight tragically sorry. I've arranged them alternately for the sake of contrast:

"Our marriage is very happy. It's a good feeling to know someone loves you and wants you, that he is working for you, building a good life for you. I wait each night for him to drive home from work."

"I have missed several years of important living: the dating period, being away from home, working and living with another girl. I wouldn't get married so young again. I'd probably marry when I'm about twenty. I was in love with him. He was anxious to get married."

"I think I would do the same thing over again. I got married because my father and I never got along well. I was unhappy and wanted to leave home."

"I don't think people should marry young. It's hard to get along when he's going to school. Our income is rather short. We probably should have waited."

"Just being together, knowing you have someone who really cares for you and that you can care for him is the most satisfying thing in our marriage. I have someone I can count on. We are independent. We have our own problems to solve."

"We've had a lot of trouble. We weren't ready for

responsibility. We shouldn't have married so young. We should have waited until after high school at least. We thought we were in love. We would get married and have good times. We had a very poor idea of what marriage was. We thought we could come and go, do as we pleased, do or not do the dishes but it isn't that way."

"No, our marriage wasn't a mistake. I'd have it just the way it was. He felt we'd been going together for so long there was no reason why we shouldn't get married now. He has wanted me to marry him for three years. I thought we should wait until he finished school and the service. We'd planned on a later wedding but we decided to get married now."

"I wouldn't marry so young. I would finish high school first. I thought I loved him. I wasn't much interested in school. I wanted to get away from home. My stepfather never showed any real interest in me.

"We are very happy keeping house. I enjoy being on my own, having the responsibility of my own place instead of being responsible to someone else."

"I wouldn't advise going steady so young. I had to get married. We would have gotten married anyway— but later. We agreed it was the right thing to do under the circumstances."

"I'm happier now because of the security we have. I didn't want to wait for three years while he was in the

Army. Even if I went to college, I couldn't have gotten anything out of it. Now I can help keep him up on his studying. He is still looking forward to going to college."

"I would like to go to college. If I had thought of college then, I wouldn't have gotten married. I guess because I loved him. He wanted me to finish high school but we were equally anxious to get married so we did."

"I got married to have a place of my own where I could relax. I wanted to have peace of mind. I have been very happy and we have gotten along just perfect."

"I would have waited a little longer until he was more mature and until I was at least eighteen or until I had a chance to work for a while. He and I didn't want to go back to school. He had a job so we decided to get married then."

"I would still get married. I don't think it's the best thing for everyone but if you're old enough to accept the responsibility of marriage then go ahead. I married for love."

"I would have waited to finish high school first. It has tied me down so. I've had no fun since I was married. I can't go to dances. I don't feel right there. The same is true about other school activities. I guess I thought he was the only one in the world. I was badly mixed up."

8

IS IT NOW—OR NEVER?

"It's tough to be alone on a shelf . . . " is a line from
an old song that seems to haunt most teen-age girls.
The current feeling is there's not a moment to lose and
it's a matter of marrying now—or never! In many high
schools if you're not engaged by graduation day, you're

ipso facto an old maid. Is it really so?

High school senior girls are a whirlpool of mixed emotions. You're thrilled to be in your final year of schooling, enjoying the respect of the younger students and the privileges of the social events that are part of the graduating year. Yet, strangely enough, you dread graduation, too. It means leaving the known and plunging into the unknown. It means leaving the established procedures of social life, work life and home life. It offers the choice of striking out as an individual, finding a job and accepting a position as an adult in adult society, or of getting married at once and being part of a twosome making your way together in the adult world. Why do so many high school girls consider marriage the only choice?

At a time when movies and TV glorify the glamour girl as the one who gets everything in life, especially the man she wants, many girls who are pleasant looking but not beauties feel they'd better grab while the grabbing's good because they may not get another chance.

A freckle-faced fourteen-year-old said, "I'm the Nothing Type. I'll be lucky if anybody wants to marry me!" With that attitude she'll probably marry the first one who asks her, grateful for his charity instead of proudly making her own selection of a husband.

As far as looks are concerned, the self-styled Nothing Types of today are often the raging beauties of tomorrow. A glimpse at any old movie magazine will confirm this. For instance, Sophia Loren who was called a skinny stick before her figure blossomed.

The Nothing Type who sees no future for herself obviously won't get much or give much to marriage either. She's defeated before she begins. Instead of seeking to improve herself, she's out to sell herself to the first buyer. In the course of marriage, she may develop and find she's dissatisfied with her hasty marriage. Even worse, she may settle into a lifetime stupor and never bother arousing herself, which is not only a suffocating way to exist but can leave her miles behind a husband who is growing and developing as a person.

If you secretly think you're a Nothing Type, make a solemn vow not to marry the first man who comes along. Vow further to become a Something Type and marry when the real man comes along.

Another source of the Marriage Panic is the so-called male shortage. That all the good men marry young is a popular misconception, often based on the fact that so many school heroes do marry at graduation. The football captain, the class president frequently marry their steady in a burst of publicity, although what's forgotten is that most BMOC's go on to college, married or not, on athletic scholarships or with special grants on the basis of scholastic ratings. Because they do often marry young does not mean they're not sorry a year later. However, the very qualities that made them school leaders gives them the additional strength and perseverance to include marriage in their busy lives.

What About Teen-Age Marriage?

The term "Male Shortage" is phony. There's no such thing because there are too many men and too many women for us to worry about a minor discrepancy one way or the other. Statistics are a seesaw of misapplied information. Marriage availability statistics are completely worthless because they can't possibly cover the men and women who chose the Church instead of marriage, the mental misfits who will never marry, the homosexuals and lesbians who forfeit their places in the marriage mart. Statisticians may shriek that these discordant notes cancel themselves out. My feeling is you're not marrying a statistic, you are marrying one man, and unless you live on some remote island off the Scottish coast where the population consists of two lighthouse keepers and one goat, chances are you will meet a great many single men and will find a husband among them.

After the age of thirty, it is true that your chances of marrying diminish but this gives you a good twelve to fifteen years to find just the right man. Among the well-known late starters are Princess Margaret who was twenty-nine at her marriage and whose husband, a glamorous and successful photographer, was the same age. Another Margaret, former President Truman's daughter, was older—thirty-two—when she married another glamorous man, newspaperman Clifton Daniel, who was thirty-eight.

The good ones don't all get carried away young. Many successful men devote their early years to building their careers, working hard for success, and then look around for a suitable wife to climb the rest of the way with them, equipped to face competition with them.

Competition is something you may shy away from. Early marriage may be the easy way out but it's a pretty sad victory, like swimming the length of the kiddy pool.

Aiming low offers little ultimate satisfaction. Not wanting to lose is understandable, but not wanting to take the chance of losing confines you to a small, airless prison.

I certainly wouldn't go so far as to say losing is fun. But losing out on something of value gives you experience that helps you win the next time the gold ring comes around. Sports stars know the value of competition. You don't win the Women's Singles at Forest Hills without working up to it. You don't feel confident with men of stature unless you've mingled with people of the same caliber.

A vital quality that is sacrificed on the altar of early marriage is independence. In order to be a successful partner in a twosome, you have to be a whole human being by yourself. Marriage should be two individuals who choose to walk together, rather than one dragging along in the shadow of the other or both leaning so completely on each other that if one tripped both would fall.

Teen-agers feel a terrible need to belong with someone. The children they see all have parents looking after them. The adults they see all seem to have mates, to do things in pairs. No longer children, on the brink of being adults, they may wish to hasten the process by adopting quickly the adult mode of life, namely marriage.

Some teen-agers do mature early, are ready for adult living and can take on marriage. What are these teen-agers like? And are you one of them?

Can you make decisions without asking all your friends what they think?

Are you able to handle money?

Do you feel qualified to earn your own living if you want to, or have to?

Have you enjoyed housekeeping when your mother was away?

If you answer Yes to these questions then you obviously have an independent spirit which would add much to a marriage.

Hand-in-glove with Independence is Self-Confidence. The two go together and enable you to become a happy, fulfilled person, whether married or single.

Marriage should not mean the end of making decisions, but rather the beginning.

Develop your self-confidence. Get into the habit of having firm opinions. If you can't make up your mind about having onions on your hamburger, or wearing a red dress to a party or studying bookkeeping, you are hardly in a position to decide on a husband and all the thousands of details that make a home.

Perhaps the idea of marriage flatters you because for the first time a man urgently, openly, warmly loves and wants you. At first it's hard to believe, and even harder to resist. You've read about love, heard about love, dreamed about love. And now it's happened. You're thrilled, excited. The phone rings. The doorbell rings. Sweet words. Gifts. Promises. Exhortations. So *this* is what life is all about! A man who thinks every breath you take is perfumed, every word you whisper a gem, everything you do a delight.

Well, then. How do you feel? If you truly feel the same way about him, then the chances are you're really in love. It *is* the most wonderful thing that's ever happened to you, so enjoy the adoration but don't get swept into marriage. Remember that it's nice to be put up on a pedestal, but once you're married you'll be expected to jump down. Unless you truly love and respect your husband, you won't find this very palatable.

If you've been worried about your future, convinced that marriage is a question of NOW—or NEVER, revise your thinking to LATER AND FOREVER.

9

WELL, WE CAN ALWAYS GET A DIVORCE....

"What'll we do this weekend?"

"I dunno. Why don't we get married?"

"Married? My parents would have a fit."

"Mine, too. So what! Let's do it anyway."

"Okay. If it doesn't work, we can always get a divorce."

While this conversation may be slightly exaggerated, it illustrates the haphazard attitude many young people have about marriage. Of course few couples are quite so outspoken in this attitude but when questioned separately, many engaged couples confessed that they thought getting married was a very exciting idea and if it didn't turn out that way, well, there was always divorce.

Religious considerations aside, divorce is not very pleasant. It can be compared to an operation. A great deal of pain and suffering leads up to it and the recuperation period is often much longer than expected—with the patient suffering from depression and a terrible sense of futility over all the time wasted and opportunities missed.

What most people seem to forget is that getting married for kicks, with the idea of a divorce always a possibility, takes you out of the marriage market. You are a married woman and while men may hang around you at parties or on the beach, they are paying court to a safely hitched filly. The quick divorce, you think, will then make you available for a bigger and better conquest, but many girls have found, to their dismay, that once free, the men who were dancing attendance have suddenly disappeared—probably to the feet of another married woman.

Despite the romantic gaiety of divorcées from the Hollywood Set who manage to change husbands every few seasons, most divorced girls find it hard to attract the kind of man they want for a second chance at matrimony. Most serious-minded young men—and they make the best husbands—are a bit leery of girls who have married so young and so foolishly.

"I don't want a starlet," remarked a twenty-five-year-old architect, single but anxious to marry. "I want a wife with her head on her shoulders. I've met a few girls of twenty and twenty-one who've already gone through one husband. They scare me!"

Divorce at any age is a tragedy. With very young couples, it is a disaster. It destroys self-confidence. It leaves a sense of failure. It creates a depressing uncertainty over the future. If there are children, they are living proof of a thoughtless, foolish mistake, forever making you a mother so you cannot go back to being a girl.

The attitudes of friends and family toward a divorcée can be hard to take.

"Of course, my family was very upset," one girl recalls. "They blamed the whole thing on me, kept telling me how stupid I was and that I would never learn to do the right thing. They watched me like a hawk. Where was I going? What time was I coming home? They kept saying they didn't want me to get myself into trouble again. I wanted to move into my own apartment or take a room somewhere and they said what would their friends say! A divorced girl living alone is like being a prostitute. Nobody respects you."

The lack of respect is hardest to take. Divorced girls

soon find out that the men they meet—married and single—view them as pushovers, an easy target for a cheap romance.

"Because I was married, they know I'm not a virgin and they keep after me. All they can say is—what have I got to lose? It's like a nightmare. Even the men in my office won't leave me alone since my divorce. I'm sorry I told anybody. I've made up my mind, the next time I meet someone I like, I'm not going to tell him about my divorce until I'm sure he wants me for me."

Other women consider divorcées a danger to them and often make things difficult from sheer self-protection. At a recent party, I watched an attractive young wife who in turn was watching her husband dance with a recently divorced neighborhood girl. Suddenly, the wife disentangled her husband, announced she had a headache and took him away from the party. The divorcée not only looked bewildered but felt terribly alone as all the other women zealously protected "their property" from this "new threat" who probably hadn't been to a party in weeks.

A good rule to remember if you are considering marriage is, "If you have doubts—don't!" Marrying with divorce as an escape route almost certainly defeats it from the start. When you anticipate failure, you generally get it. Marriage to combat loneliness will only prove that two can be as miserable as one and that the inevitable divorce must leave deep scars on the two victims.

Don't be swept away by Marriage Fever either. "Always a bridesmaid, never a bride" may ring in your ears after attending several weddings, and you might feel that with everybody else doing it, why not you? The reason is that marriage is not a new hobby, a dance craze or a way-out hair style to try once and forget if dissatisfied.

Also responsible for many divorces is the mistaken notion that the quarrels and misgivings you have beforehand will magically fade away *after* you're married, the most common and saddest epitaph for a dead marriage.

Marriage may be an institution but it is not a reform school. Personality differences, character traits, things "you haven't even discussed because you don't want to fight" are not going to magically work themselves out after the wedding. The time to get everything out in the open is before you sign the contract, not after it's signed, sealed and delivered.

Following are some of the essential points on which you and your husband should agree, or be willing to accept each other's viewpoint.

MONEY: How you will use your income. More on clothes, less on food? A certain amount set aside for vacations? A Baby Fund? Do you think the apartment comes first while he thinks the money should go to buy a car? Who will take care of the household money? You? He? Both? Will you get an allowance for running the household or will bills be paid as they come in? If you work, will your salary go straight into the bank and you both live on his earnings?

Money as the root of all evil is one of the understatements of all time. It creates more bad feeling and petty hatreds than sex and mother-in-laws combined.

CHILDREN: How many do you want—and how soon? Are you prepared to put aside money for them and provide living space for them? Does your husband-to-be really like children or does he consider them your department, to take care of and nurture while he simply admires the results? Having a baby at seventeen or eighteen on a limited income, with a husband who doesn't help with the care and feeding, but regards the baby as a doll, can be very embittering for an inexperienced wife. Discuss all your feelings about children beforehand. You may dissolve a marriage but you can't dissolve children.

SEX: This, of course, is difficult to discuss but an attempt should be made. You won't know what your ultimate sexual adjustments will be until many months after marriage, but be as honest as possible with yourself at the outset.

You may admire a man and be thrilled at his wanting to marry you but, secretly, you may not feel a great physical excitement for him. While sexual attraction should not be the sole basis of marriage, it is vitally necessary to its success. You may say to yourself, "He's wonderful. I love him. But I don't like the way he kisses —or having his hands on me."

Experts tell us that when sexual relations between man and woman are good, other problems can generally be worked out and sex is not of topmost importance. But when the physical relationship between two people is bad, then everything else becomes tainted with ill-feeling and recrimination.

If you are disgusted or frightened or unhappy about any part of your physical relationship with your future husband or if any of his physical habits offend you, don't let them slide. Awkward as it may be, talk them over. Once the barriers are down, you may find there are some things you do that irritate or upset him, too.

You may detect a note of cruelty in his love-making that vaguely frightens you. With the fuller intimacy of marriage, things won't get better; they'll get worse.

FAMILY RELATIONSHIPS: "Before we were married, my husband said he hated family get-togethers and I didn't think much about it. Now, I'm miserable. I'm not a mamma's girl but we've been married two years and Ralph has refused to visit them once, not even at Christmas when I had to deliver our presents all by myself. My folks aren't the interfering kind but their feelings are hurt and so are mine."

SOCIAL LIFE: He hates to wear a tie; you love to wear cocktail dresses. He prefers the mountains; you love the seashore. He wants to spend a couple of evenings a week with "the boys" and expects you to stay home being a good wife. He thinks dances and picnics are for kids; you think they're fun, and you want to go.

These are basic differences. If you are diametrically opposed on matters of fun, vacations and social activity, giving in or compromising won't really solve anything. Resentment is certain to crop up sooner or later.

HAVE SECOND THOUGHTS IF:

You love going out with a crowd once in a while and he prefers fiddling with the hi-fi by himself.

You're extremely neat and he's a galloping slob.

You are always on time and he's always late.

You don't like to drink and he thinks bar-hopping is the only way to spend an evening out.

You think he's much sexier than you.

You don't like his friends and he doesn't like yours.

Divorce is a sad situation. The facts about divorce are even sadder. According to Katherine Oettinger, director of the United States Children's Bureau, there are more than fifteen thousand divorced teen-age girls in the country at this moment.

Divorce may seem easy, widespread, an escape hatch, but as viewed by Domestic Relations Court Judge Willard Gatling, "I wish every student could spend one day in my court. We see nothing here but broken hearts."

10

TWO CAN LIVE AS CHEAPLY AS ONE—IF ONE DOESN'T EAT

The best things in life may be free, but if you use this philosophy in the supermarket you're liable to wind up behind bars. If you haven't been inside a supermarket recently, take a test run through your mother's local favorite. Either use her shopping list or pretend that you are buying a few days' provisions for yourself and your future husband.

Milk. Meat. Eggs. Fruit. Vegetables. Cookies. Jam. Spaghetti. Bread. Ice cream. Butter. Cheese. And that's only the beginning. What about soaps, cleansers, detergents, polishes and so on? This will give you some advance idea of only one segment of your married budget.

If you've been used to clomping your way through the refrigerator at the slightest inner twinge, you may be in for a slight shock when you find out how much it costs to nourish a healthy teen-ager. And it takes twice as much food to nourish two healthy just-marrieds.

Money talks before marriage will save you money aches afterward. Make a list of all continuing household and personal expenses. These will include: Food. Rent. Gas and Electricity. Telephone. Payments on furniture or appliances such as a TV. Insurance or payments for medical or health plans. Dental Care. Clothing. Personal needs, toiletries, etc. Entertainment. Transportation. Vacation Fund.

Add them up to arrive at an approximate cost of your month's basic expenses. Then add up what your income will be. Do the two figures coincide? Is your income bigger than your basic outgo? If it is, you are in good shape—and very unusual, too. If you've always been vague about your allowance, wondering where it all went, you will have to make a special effort to keep track of your expenses and allot your household income to cover all of them.

Managing household expenses is like any other game of skill. You have to learn all the rules and then practice constantly for perfection. You can also learn much from your parents. What kind of a roast goes further? How to organize your check book. Whether it's better to take out one large bank loan to finance all your household purchases, pay a monthly installment on each item separately or save up for each luxury and buy it outright.

In some teen-age marriages, the parents are willing to subsidize the young couple while they continue their schooling. Often the wife will drop out of school to have a baby or to help toward supporting her husband while he acquires the training necessary for a good future income.

In rare cases, where parents are wealthy, the newly-weds can be set up in their own apartment, with an allowance provided to pay all their expenses. In this ideal arrangement, both can go to school, dividing up the chores of cooking and cleaning between them according to their schedules. If they attend a university, they may live in the Married Undergraduates quarters provided by many schools, or rent a furnished room off campus and have their meals out.

In most cases, however, subsidy is partial. The couple lives with one or the other set of parents, the husband works full or part-time depending on his schooling. The parents may ask for a small contribution to the household or may regard this as their contribution to the marriage until it can stand alone.

As for the ticklish problem of whether or not to live with either set of parents, Dr. Rebecca Liswood emphatically states, "I honestly feel it is very bad for a young couple to live with the family, or even close by. There are too many adjustments for a young couple to make without the added complication of parents. For something as simple as a quarrel, you should have complete privacy—to fight and forgive, with no outside interference.

"If parents are willing and able to subsidize you, ask them to give you a weekly allowance or 'salary' so that you can budget your money yourselves and learn to live within your 'income.' If parents just pay your bills, without your having any responsibility for managing your own finances, you will have very little feeling of being married."

Frequently, Dr. Liswood points out, a young couple will accept a "loan" from their parents to carry them through until the young husband's earning capacity is big enough to start paying the money back. Financial independence from parents is a big factor toward emotional independence as well.

As a typical example, Joe and Betty moved into Joe's old room in his family's New York apartment, pushing out Joe's younger brother who had to sleep on a couch in the dining room. From the start, the situation was a bad one. The little brother, peeved at being displaced, complained that Betty used up all the tooth paste and ate all the cookies. Joe's mother kept circling ads in the newspapers for jobs which Betty might take instead of going to school. Joe's father boasted about how he was "taking care of the children," which infuriated Betty because her parents had continued her allowance to help the couple get along.

Within six months, they moved into a furnished room. "We lived on spaghetti, beans and hope until Joey finished school. My mother used to send me 'Care' packages of roasted chickens and chocolate brownies. Then we'd have a feast. I never realized living cost so much."

Parents have conflicting views on the subject. Some feel that marriage is an adult institution which should not be entered into unless you are an adult and can pay your own way. Others take the view that two young people in love should be able to start living together as soon as they feel ready, and that if the boy wants to continue his education, the least they as parents can do is help out in the early stages.

Where parents are unwilling—or financially unable —to contribute support, the teen-age wife may decide to quit school and work while her husband finishes his training. In many cases, this is a noble expression of love and confidence on her part. Many successful doctors, lawyers, architects and other professional men owe their achievements to loyal wives who worked to support them while they studied. However, in most of these cases, the wives did finish high school and gave up the thought of college to help their husbands. Where many recent marriages have gone wrong is where the wife leaves high school before graduation.

There are emotional as well as financial factors which say, "Don't do it!" Financially, without a high school diploma your earnings are on a rock-bottom level. You may not care at the moment, but if you continue working you will find yourself passed over for promotion or simply not considered for responsible jobs. Looking ahead, when the children start school you may want to go back to work,and once again the stigma of "no diploma" will keep you from truly gainful employment.

Emotionally this will affect your confidence, too. You may feel intellectually inferior to your husband and secretly—if not openly—blame him for limiting your horizons. Because of his advanced education he may not be able to help looking down his nose at you. There will be subjects he'll want to discuss which you know nothing about, areas of interest you may never have heard mentioned. Later, too, you may feel at a disadvantage with your children, ashamed of being un-educated, wary of teaching them anything in case it should be incorrect.

Have you ever heard the song, "Put that ring on my finger. Put that piece of paper in my hand." Every bride should not only have a ring and a license, but another piece of paper, too—a high school diploma.

If your husband quits school, you may be in for the kind of trouble that neither one of you will ever admit to each other since the fault will lie on both your heads for ever allowing him to do it. A man without a high school diploma almost surely cuts his lifetime earnings in half. The first job is easy to get. If you both work at the start, your combined earnings may be as high as $125 a week, but with the first baby, your income is cut in half while your expenses are doubled. Of course, your husband can continue school at night and work part-time, a backbreaking schedule that is hard on the nerves and the health.

Where working, schooling and being married are combined, you face the multiple problem of adequate living conditions, nutritious food and a happy personal relationship. More than at any time in your married life, you will have to give each other patience, tenderness and understanding.

Though each case history is different, they all seem to pivot on stamina. You must analyze the financial aspects of your marriage, decide on whether you can meet the demands of marital upkeep and then if you take the plunge, keep a stiff upper lip while you fight for survival.

You haven't counted on a baby. Your plan is to work for two years, then start a family. But it didn't happen that way and you had to quit your job after a year. So your financial situation is not good.

Some resourceful young mothers have managed to add to their income in different ways. One young mother fixed up their back yard with several playpens and rented out "parking rights" to other mothers who wanted to shop for a few hours or have their hair done without worrying about the Baby. She earned pin money this way and what's more, adored the work.

Another young mother oiled up her sewing machine and spread the word that she was taking orders for curtains, table mats and other household items. She built up quite an enjoyable trade which not only gave her plenty of company when neighbors called but a substantial income, too.

Sewing is one of the best skills you can have for cutting expenses. If you can alter clothes, make some of them, run up your own towels, aprons, curtains, and later on, your baby's things, you save a considerable amount and are putting one of your talents to good use.

You can save money, too, by learning to do your own painting and repairing. If you and your husband can change the cord on the iron, take the toaster apart, unclog the sink, refinish an old chest, you needn't spend time or go to the expense of finding people to do these chores.

If you're both rusty along these lines, make it a point to start learning how to "do it yourself." This is a modern age. Many things work by pushing a button. When you push the button and nothing happens, then what? Back to the pioneer days and the need to do things with your own two hands.

As mentioned earlier, the job you take as a teen-ager may not have much future, but as a means to an end it can contribute much toward meeting expenses. The problem, then, is choosing the right job; that is, the job that will best fit into your schedule as a married woman. Choose carefully, looking for a position that will best suit you in terms of convenience and experience. You want a job that is easy to get to, perhaps with shopping facilities nearby. You want a job that won't demand too much of your wardrobe or your energy. You want a job that you can leave promptly at closing time so that you can get home for supper preparation. You want a job that is stimulating but not exhausting.

You want a job that will teach you something. Selling in a shop will acquaint you with the various values of merchandise. Working in an office will teach you efficiency and organization which can be translated into valuable time and space savers at home. Supervising children in a playground will give you lots of fresh air to offset the weekend indoors when you will have to do the heavy cleaning, ironing, etc, as well as helping your husband with his studies.

That love and marriage go together like a horse and carriage may not be denied, but before you start off down that open road be sure you have somewhere to sleep.

11

BUT WHAT IF I DON'T MARRY NOW? WHAT HAPPENS IF I WAIT?

Burl Ives sings a folk song about a teen-age girl who tells her mother she thinks it's time she married because "for fourteen long years, I've been livin' all alone."

You may feel that fourteen, or sixteen or even eighteen isn't quite long enough for you to be single and that you'd like to explore life, see a few things on your own before settling down to home, husband and children. But you might be worried about the uncertainty. If the ambition of most of your friends seems to be marriage as soon as possible, you may be wondering what will happen to you if you do decide to wait a few years.

What is life like as a loner—the joys and rewards of the bachelor girl, the advantages or disadvantages of making decisions by and for yourself? The sometimes exciting, sometimes bewildering problem of MEN and how to separate the wolves from the lambs?

If you've thought about marriage—and who hasn't? —and you're not completely sold on being a twosome just yet, why not try flying solo. Testing your own wings, taking a chance on soaring high or falling flat on your face the first time may change your entire perspective and you may find your nesting place in some previously unheard of roost.

As a teen-ager and a student, you've lived and worked as part of a group, in your family and at school. If you've been going steady, your social life has likewise been a matter of joint decisions.

It can be a little scary being your own boss but it can also be very sweet. Whether its a job, a man, a decision, the key to your development is that word ADULT. On the job, your success depends on how quickly you catch onto the work, how responsible you are about arriving on time, executing your assignments efficiently, co-operating well with others. There's no homework, no report cards, nobody after you to do this or that. The stakes are not a good report card; they are salary increases, job promotions and the satisfaction of doing something well.

The yen to be independent doesn't mean breaking family ties or forgetting family obligations. The family unit is a precious thing and a strong bulwark to have behind you as you go out into the world. Most parents will encourage your move toward independence, fully prepared to help you take the plunge. Often they may offer suggestions and warnings you think corny, but don't close your ears to all of them. Older people may "not understand" exactly what's going on at your job or among your roommates but somewhere in their advice may be a nugget or two of truth that will serve you well. Talking and listening are two of the most helpful habits you can acquire, keeping close connections with your family the most rewarding resolve you can make.

The Joys and Rewards of the Bachelor Girl are many. With a job, you have a chance to mingle with older, successful men and women, to hear their opinions, listen to their viewpoints, to learn by example things which may include everything from operating a difficult machine to placing an order by telephone and dressing in a way that is both neat and pretty.

Having your first job when you are young offers many advantages. Errors and uncertainty are almost expected from you because of your youth and are for-given accordingly. In large offices and factories, new girls are looked after with care.

You will be earning money and meeting new people. You will undoubtedly be changing your appearance. It's happened to others. Think of that girl in your neigh-borhood—maybe the older sister of a friend—who worked for a year in Chicago. When she returned, she was so improved that nobody recognized her!

As a Bachelor Girl, you develop a sense of style, a feeling for clothes, hair styling, make-up keyed to your new life. You learn by experiment what is flattering to your figure, your coloring, the shape of your face and head. You walk differently, talk differently, act differ-ently from the way you did at school. Your horizons are wider. The world is a big place—and with a job you have the money to see some of it.

You can take a weekend trip, save toward a car, collect special bits for your hope chest even though you may not be opening it for a while.

Where you live depends of course on the job oppor-tunities near home and whether or not you have a hankering to see another part of the country. Living at home may be more comfortable and will enable you to save more of your earnings, although it may take some time for your family to stop thinking of you as a school-girl.

If you decide to try a big city, have some money saved up and a place to stay before you start out. The

Y.W.C.A. or a recognized Girls' Residence Club are the best places to use as home base while job-hunting. They can also advise you on how to share an apartment with some other girls. Above all, don't think of moving into a furnished room by yourself. Not only is it expensive but you will be swamped with loneliness and you will be sought after by unpleasant men on the prowl for naïve young things. Sharing an apartment is fun. If some girls you knew at school have the same idea in mind, then you can take an apartment together. Otherwise, newspapers in big cities are full of ads looking for one more girl to share an apartment which one member has left—usually to get married.

Sharing an apartment gives you the company of girls your own age with whom you can discuss problems and ambitions, also a chance for joint entertaining, cooking, shopping for food and making ends meet on a budget. Your interests will broaden because you'll be close to the interests of others. Mary is mad on jazz; Mimi goes to modeling school and works part-time as a receptionist; Jeannie is a stewardess and brings home strange concoctions from around the world; Phyllis cooks the best spaghetti sauce this side of Italy and Barbara adores giving home permanents.

As for meeting people socially, sharing an apartment is sure fire. Everyone's friends meet everyone else's and by holding open house every so often, you can invite people you don't know too well to just drop in. Sharing gives you the freedom for entertaining and the safety of numbers.

Although sharing an apartment means sharing expenses and responsibilities for household chores, you nonetheless control your own destiny. If you don't like your roommates, or the way they conduct themselves, you can always leave. If your job isn't working out, you can always make a change. You can go out with a different boy every night or fall in love with a new man right away or keep in touch with your high school sweetheart and perhaps decide, after all, that he is surely the one for you.

Having a job and living on your own salary are worthwhile experiences because they teach you the value of money, what it can buy, how to make it go furthest and best. Once you've worked, this counts as valuable experience if you decide to earn some money after the baby is born or even much later when the children start school and you have several hours a day to put to good use.

The question of Sex and the Bachelor Girl is, as always, a tricky one. To begin with, you must accept the fact that you are and should behave as an adult. By this I don't mean tumbling into the arms of any man who shows you some attention. However, now that you are a working girl you can't put men off with the "But I'm only a schoolgirl" defense.

The Battle of the Sexes is aptly named. Men do chase girls. Many men do have but one thing in mind—and that usually is not marriage. It may be unfair, but you must face the fact that you are fair game and must stick to your principles of behavior no matter what.

Unfair, too, but equally factual is the vulnerability of girls. You, not the men, are in danger of acquiring a cheap reputation, and worse, to be blunt, of becoming pregnant. There's always lots of talk about "The Double Standard" *vs.* "The Single Standard." If men can live freely, have love affairs before marriage, why not women, too? The answer is simple. Women are not men.

If you have the guts to give up the rights and protection and prerogatives of being a female, then go to it. But when it comes to marriage, men will regard you as a "good sport" and a great girl to take away on weekends but not much of a prospect as a wife. To live on the Single Standard means to live, figuratively, as a man, taking your chances in the rough-and-tumble of sexual irresponsibility. You can't expect men to have respect for you as a woman if you have no regard for yourself as one.

The bane of every career girl's existence is the Older and usually Married Man. He may be sophisticated. He may be fatherly. He may remind you of John Wayne, which is like being the most glamorous grandfather in the world. And indeed, he may be all these things though I doubt it.

You may meet him where you work, or at a party, or someone may have asked him to your apartment. If he takes an interest in you, be friendly but firm. Let him know that the only married men you go out with are father, brothers and uncles, all your own. Period.

Your job may prove more interesting than you expected and may suddenly open a brand new career for you while you're still young enough to acquire the training and experience to make it an important one. A friend of mine became an assistant salesgirl in a department store because it was the first ad she saw the day after graduation. After three months of learning the ropes, she became fired with the idea of being a buyer. She took several night school courses in merchandising, retailing and fashions while keeping her daytime job. Now, at the age of twenty-five, she has an exciting life as a buyer, travels to Europe twice a year and earns a fabulous salary. Last year, in Paris, she met a young and equally successful fabric designer and two months later they got married. She plans to quit her job when their first baby is born, although the store has told her there is always a job for her when she wants it.

Night courses not only increase your earning power but also enlarge your circle of acquaintances. Many romances have begun in evening classes, the desire for self-improvement being part of the mutual attraction. Courses are valuable to your future marriage, too. Bookkeeping keeps the checkbook straight and tells you in advance what you can spend on your vacation. Interior decorating and dressmaking help you express your ideas and the sewing machine saves money. As you can see, the possibilities are endless.

Travel is one of the most gratifying experiences I know, and as a Bachelor Girl you have the money and the opportunity to travel. Most boys may complain about their compulsory military service but they all agree that seeing new places and meeting new people with new ideas have enriched their lives.

With organized tours and budget travel schemes, a two-week vacation can take you to Europe, Asia, or South America or anywhere in the United States. A weekend can be spent in nearby places of interest. If you have friends or relatives in places you've never seen, this is the time to visit them, as a Bachelor Girl with your eyes wide open, ready and able to meet experience head on.

A girl of twenty-five told me, "I've been married ten years but I don't feel as if I've ever lived! Do you know I've never even taken a train trip by myself?"

A twenty-year-old divorcée explained, "I couldn't stand being married any longer. As far as I'm concerned, the past three years have been a waste of time. I should have been going places, meeting people and doing things. Instead, I was home making beds!"

Gadding about. Traveling. Changing jobs. Going to parties. Dating men. Frivolous? Perhaps, but every bit of it is a learning experience. Gadding about gives you poise and confidence that last a lifetime. Traveling stimulates ideas and gives you something to tell your children. Changing jobs gives you adaptability to new surroundings and new responsibilities. Lots of parties and lots of men provide gaiety and new faces from which to choose whatever suits you—from a new way to wear your hair to a suitable husband.

These, in their special way, are insurance for a future happy marriage. Even in the most devoted families, you may have moments of restlessness or depression, but if you can look back on your Bachelor Girl days and assess them for exactly what they were, you will realize how much more satisfying it is to be married. If you've never known the exultation of youthful freedom, your marriage may crack up on the rocks of self-recrimination and longing for what you've missed.

What are the most boring questions a Bachelor Girl gets asked?

"Will you come up to my apartment?" is one.

"Don't you trust me?" is another.

While these two are certain to arouse a sickly smile of recognition on your face, the most irritating and hardest to answer is the old, "So when are you getting married?"

How to handle the intense interest in this vital question by family and married friends is a continuing chore for Bachelor Girls. Those who are married, you will find, are dedicated missionaries to the cause of bundling you to the altar as quickly as possible. Run into married friends with a man and next day they're on the phone congratulating you. Write to your parents about being given a box of chocolates and the next thing you know your mother's pricing wedding cakes.

Needling from the side lines may precipitate a marriage that had barely reached the talk stage and might better have been left there. Remember, whatever the pressures of friends and family, there are only two people directly concerned with your marriage. You and your husband. You will have to live with each other, work out your problems, make sacrifices and compromises for each other's sake. Once the Marriage-Makers have rushed you to the altar, their job is done, they're off looking for other culprits, and you're on your own.

As for your chances of getting married after twenty-one, they are only a fraction smaller than during your teens for one obvious reason. Some of the men are already married but the field is not only still very big—but so much better because it's more selective. A man in his mid-twenties to mid-thirties has become set in his character and direction so you can judge the kind of a man he already is—rather than the kind of man he might grow up to be.

Being a Bachelor Girl for a few years can be a healthy, exhilarating period of your life. It is not by any wild stretch of imagination meant to be a substitute for marriage. Rather, it should be a profitable link between being a student and becoming a wife.

12

BEING MARRIED SOUNDS AWFUL! AM I NORMAL?

You've heard it said. You've read about it. You've seen it among your friends. Some girls grow up more quickly than others. Joan may marry at sixteen, have a baby at seventeen and be ecstatically happy, whereas Jane at fifteen may still seem a child with only a passing interest in boys and only a mild desire to make love.

Perhaps you are more of a Jane than a Joan. Perhaps you've been secretly worried that you're undersexed, that you think kissing and necking are okay but you would be happier if you didn't have to do it, that you like boys and may even be going steady because that's the only way to have a good time at school, that you accept this because kissing one boy is better than kissing lots of them.

When your girl friends sit around and talk about sex, marriage and having babies, you feel even more worried because the whole thing sounds awful and you're sure you don't want anything to do with it.

A fifteen-year-old confided, "I don't want to get married. I don't want to sleep with a man. Is there something wrong with me? Am I abnormal or something?"

If you feel the same at twenty-four, then it's time to be concerned because it means your instincts have not fully developed.

But in your teens, maturity does not blossom at the same rate in everyone. Your body and your emotions develop in spurts. Your figure changes almost overnight. You may grow two inches in two months. And then, gradually or quite suddenly, you feel an overpowering surge of emotional desire for the opposite sex. You become modest in front of your father and brothers. You enjoy holding hands with a boy. You want him to kiss you and touch you. In this development of sexual feeling, you might even enjoy fighting with boys, wrestling becomes very exciting, any physical contact with the opposite sex has a new stimulation.

These changes may begin gradually at twelve or thirteen and reach maturity at fifteen or sixteen. On the other hand, they may not begin until fourteen or fifteen and may not reach maturity until seventeen or eighteen. Remember, the slow starters get there just the same!

An example of Slow Starters is the mousy girl who never said boo to anyone or had a date in high school. After a year at college, she was elected Freshman Queen and was engaged by the end of her sophomore year. There was the sixteen-year-old who vowed she would never marry because she couldn't stand having a boy kiss her. At twenty-two, she's happily married with two children.

Many boys mature slowly, too. Successful men in their thirties will admit they never kissed a girl until they were eighteen, didn't fall in love until they were twenty-one. How often have you noticed the fantastic difference in a boy after a summer away or a few months in one of the services?

Don't feel foolish if you honestly think your education, your hobbies or training for a career are more important than going steady or necking in a car. Don't worry about being a square. Athletics, dramatics, designing your own clothes, working as a nurse's aide will not only make you a more interesting and well-rounded person but will add enormously to the success of your eventual marriage.

As for boys, you don't have to hide or avoid them completely. "But if I don't want to neck, they won't want to be with me!" you may protest. This is true only to a point. Boys are caught up in the social scheme of things just as much as girls. While they naturally have sexual drives, they think that being a Sex Machine is expected of them, that if they don't try to kiss a girl she'll think there's something wrong.

You can enjoy the company of boys without being physical and you'll find that if you say, "Why don't we just talk . . . dance . . . go for a ride . . . play Ping-pong . . ." that the boy will be happy to comply. One or two may sneer or call you a baby, but don't be intimidated into doing anything you don't want to do. By pursuing your hobbies and interests, you're certain to find other boys and girls who feel as you do. There are other things in the world besides sex. One of them being Love.

True love is one of the most exquisitely delicate emotions the human being can achieve. It is a meeting and understanding of the mind, the soul and the emotions. While it is enhanced by physical expression, it should be remembered that some of the world's greatest and most enduring love affairs were completely spiritual.

13

PEN PAL ROMANCES

Remember how you used to fill in coupons and send away for sample lipsticks and how exciting it was to receive your own personal mail? And when personal mail comes from your own personal male, it's even more exciting.

Pen Pal Romances fall into two separate groups: boys you have met or know very well and who are away at school, work or one of the services; boys you've never met personally but who are friends of a brother or a cousin in some distant place.

Often, Pen Pal Friendships develop into deeply personal friendships and sometimes ripen into something more, a very special kind of closeness that is attained when inner thoughts are expressed and shared. You may be slightly tongue-tied talking to a boy face to face or on the telephone, but alone with your thoughts and pen and paper you may find yourself able to express subtle nuances of feelings and ideas. It works the other way, too. The boy who never had much more to say than "Pass the ketchup," may find letter writing an exciting and revealing way to get to know a girl.

In fact, when you think of the great love affairs of the past—before telephones—letters flew back and forth even when both lived in the same city. After marriage, too, husbands and wives left notes for each other, saying on paper the things they would not—or could not—say aloud. Because of the telephone, nobody writes letters unless distance separates them from the recipient.

But, you may ask, is it possible to fall in love through letters?

It is possible to learn a good deal about another person through letters, sometimes more than you might learn from personal meetings spent having fun, with little personal conversation. It is possible through letters to appreciate the other person's ideals, ambitions, to sympathize with his doubts, fears, to be emotionally stirred by his manliness. Many successful marriages have resulted from a long period of correspondence.

"I knew Eric for a year before he went into the Army but we really didn't have much to say to each other until he started to write to me. Soon we were writing every day, all our thoughts, our dreams, what we hated, what we liked, how we wanted to live and what kind of home and children and future we wanted. On his first leave home we got engaged, feeling as if we'd known each other for years—and everything about each other. Having written without inhibitions, we found we could talk freely and openly with each other."

A young wife who started corresponding with her future husband as a complete stranger, told me, "Mitch was my cousin's buddy in the Navy. He saw my picture and asked for my address. They were in the Far East for nearly a year and we exchanged mementos, pictures, gifts and several letters a week. After a while we talked about marriage and were unofficially engaged. When Mitch got shore leave, he brought me an engagement ring—and the minute we saw each other we knew we were right. We didn't feel like strangers at all. It was as if we'd known each other for years. We decided to wait until his discharge and six months later we got married."

The thing to remember with pen pal romances is that

falling in love by mail does not mean marrying by mail. If your marriage were a matter of two packets of love letters tied together with a marriage knot, then there would be nothing more to discuss. But married love is much more physical than printing SWAK on an envelope.

People do not always live up to the impression they convey in writing. As a disillusioned friend of mine recalled, "I wrote to a boy through a Pen Pal Club and it was all like a fairy tale. He was kind, affectionate, sensitive in his letters and his pictures were very nice, too. He wasn't handsome but he had a sweet face and big brown eyes and wavy black hair.

"At Christmas time, he came to my home town and stayed with some distant relatives. It was the worst Christmas of my life. He was so sloppy I cringed when I looked at him. His hair was all lank, his nails were caked with dirt and his clothes looked as if he'd worn them nonstop for years. I don't think he ever saw a bathtub in his life! He was pretty crude, too, trying to give me a kiss right in front of my mother the first second he was in the house. I finally had to tell him I couldn't be engaged to him and I didn't think we should write any more."

Letters can fan the spark of love but can't feed the flame all by themselves.

If you enjoy writing letters, have as many Pen Pals as you can handle. It's always fun to have friends in other places with whom you can exchange ideas and, later on, personal visits.

If the boy you are writing to is in one of the services, remember that he is lonely away from his family and friends. To him, you are a pretty young girl who cares enough to write, to send him cookies and socks, to make him feel wanted and cherished. His buddies will see your photos, hear snippets of your letters, tease him about his girl and ask him when he's going to take the plunge? So his letters to you may imply more than friendship.

To you he is a wonderful guy in uniform, traveling around, undergoing dangerous training, and you are thrilled by the glamour of his letters and by his attentions.

As noted earlier in this chapter, these are all valuable, healthy developments between two people. But don't allow them to be the sole basis for a marriage. A girl who became engaged to a sergeant in the Air Force she had never met, flew to his base to marry him after he called her up to propose. The minute they met, she knew the whole thing was a mistake but decided it was nerves and besides, her mother had warned her not to go and she couldn't go home and admit it was all a mistake. Six miserable months later, she had to admit it was a hideous mistake, one she deeply regretted, as well as the unpleasantness and costliness of the annulment that followed.

If he lives in another city, arrange to get together but

not alone. If you visit him, stay with friends or family, or travel with a close friend or relative. Don't stay with him and his family because such close quarters could be awkward. It's far better for him to visit your town if possible, although again it's better if he does not stay in your home. Your first meetings should be among family or friends so that there is less strain in seeing each other in person after an intense courtship by mail.

If you knew each other for a short time before starting to correspond—at a summer camp or on a vacation trip, for instance—guard against living on the golden image of a sun-bronzed god in tennis shorts beating you at tennis. The atmosphere of a vacation makes everyone seem different.

If you enjoy writing letters, continue to have Pen Pals. Writing will give you the opportunity to examine your own mind as well as to probe others'. One final warning, don't allow pen pal friendships to become a substitute for an active social life. Don't retire from local competition because the boys you "really like are somewhere else." Pen pal friendships usually offer only the best part of friendship. Petty annoyances, irritations, shifts in allegiance don't exist in letters. Such friendships are therefore safer and less hazardous than those conducted in person. The power of the pen is great but only goes so far. You must go the rest of the way yourself.

14

BABIES—THEY'RE NOT DOLLS

They're cuter than dolls, but they're also more demanding. You can leave a doll upside down on a chair overnight and it won't complain or be the worse for neglect. You can collect dolls and store them on a shelf or behind glass doors, and aside from an occasional dusting they're no trouble at all. But a baby becomes part of your every waking and sleeping moment almost from the very moment it is conceived.

Do you think you're ready to be a teen-age mother? What happens physically before and after you give birth? What are the emotional and psychological reactions on you and your husband? And, for that matter, your parents?

How about the financial requirements? The social limitations? And, these taken care of, the joys and satisfactions of parenthood?

The point is you might be a terrific baby-sitter but not yet ready for the full-time demands and responsibility of a baby. "I just LOVE babies," a high school junior enthused, hugging and kissing the neighbor's two moppets she was taking to the park after school. And they obviously adored her, too. She had no trouble at all feeding the infant his orange juice, wiping the three-year-old's nose, while answering his nonstop questions. From the look of things, she would make a wonderful mother. Her maternal feelings were well developed. She was tolerant of children's helplessness, agile enough to chase them, patient enough to handle their demands.

She told me she was going steady and that she and her boy friend were earning extra money from odd jobs and baby-sitting which they put in a joint bank account as their Marriage Fund. So far they had one hundred and twenty-five dollars and would keep at it until they thought they had enough.

They wanted four children, two of each kind if possible, she confessed. She didn't want an outside career. She considered homemaking and motherhood her career, marriage and babies her dream—to begin as soon as they were emotionally and financially set.

This young couple apparently have the right approach. They have a mature attitude in planning and saving toward their marriage. They have examined their feelings, not only for each other but about their life goals. As a further step in the right direction, they have enrolled in a Marriage Planning Course.

An old singsong rhyme goes, "First comes love, then comes marriage. Then comes Mom wheeling the baby carriage." And with most young people, that's exactly how it happens. As a teen-ager, your body is ready for reproduction but—are you yourself, and the person you want to marry, ready for parenthood?

If you say you'd love to have children, what are your reasons? As a test of your readiness for children of your own, answer the following questions, Yes or No.

1. Do you adore small animals?
2. Have you ever cared for a sick child?
3. Are you afraid of physical examination?
4. Do you like to do what you like to when you like to do it?
5. Would you like to have become a movie star or a famous model or an airline hostess?
6. Are you on time for appointments?

A feeling of protectiveness toward small, helpless creatures is an essential to motherhood. Of all the world's offspring, the human baby is the most helpless for the longest period of time. A newborn infant can't even turn over by itself. After being fed, it cannot even burp by itself, but must be picked up and gently patted to help its digestive system to function. To understand and cope with this complete dependency is the pleasure and responsibility you will face.

Infants do get sick, not seriously, but because of their delicate bodies, the first year is a constant war against infected ears, eyes, nose, tummy upsets and teething pains. If sickness makes you squeamish, if you lack the patience to soothe and minister, your duties as a mother will be extremely burdensome.

As for your own body, you can't be squeamish about it, either. Later in this chapter we outline completely what happens to your body from the time the baby is conceived until it is born, and as you will see, shame and fear will add problems which needn't exist at all. Before getting married it is advisable to have what doctors call a pelvic examination, that is an examination of your sexual and reproductive parts. They are your essential equipment as a wife and prospective mother and you can't ignore them as if they weren't there. You may feel "It's part of nature, it'll take care of itself," but case after case reveal minor irregularities that the doctor should have known about before a baby was started. A pelvic examination may be embarrassing at first, but remember this is the area that will contain your baby and from which it will be born, and it has to be right for the function it performs.

The last three questions are not quite as irrelevant as they seem at first glance. Wanting to do what you want to do, no matter what, is a kind of bullheadedness that may get good results with parents, friends and your husband, but just try stamping your foot at a screaming two-month-old baby. Having your own way is a luxury you must forego for the privilege of motherhood. If the baby is feverish from teething, you will have to cancel an evening out. If the baby wakes up early yelling for food, you can't say "forget it" and turn over.

During the first few years of life, a baby is completely helpless and dependent and you, in turn, must be prepared to be a combination of lady-in-waiting, slave, teething ring, crying towel and wet nurse. Its duties include answering summons before they come. The hours are long, the duties numerous, the recompense very exciting.

Having a secret ambition for a glamorous career is a normal urge in most girls' lives. If you've won a few beauty contests or sung with a local combo or modeled in a department store, you may wonder if fame and fortune are within your grasp should you have the nerve to reach for it. These secret dreams of glory become even more aggravating when the confinement of a husband, a home and a baby seem to fence you in.

A young mother, dark circles of sleepless unhappiness under her eyes, confessed, "I'm ashamed of myself but sometimes I hate the baby and wish I'd never met my husband. I'm nineteen years old and if I weren't married I'd work my way to New York and get a job in fashions. Everybody says I make beautiful clothes, but now I'll never know whether or not I could have become a great designer."

Never knowing what you might have done is what rankles. A year or two of trying your luck before marriage more than makes up for years of recrimination afterward. And if you do succeed as an actress, a model, a designer, a reporter, a secretary, nurse or anything else, you then know what you're giving up when you finally turn to motherhood. It's been said career girls enjoy marriage and motherhood more than girls who marry straight from school. They know how hard you must work to succeed. They've tasted the excitements and disappointments of the business world and now want the reality of marriage with no regrets or might-have-beens.

Reliability comes into preparation for motherhood. If you can't be on time for appointments, if your homework is always late, if you think rules are for other people, you will find motherhood a nightmare. During pregnancy your body must be maintained like a delicate precision instrument. You must watch your weight and adhere to the diet given you by the doctor, and you must keep your appointments with the doctor because not only will you jeopardize your health through neglect but most gynecologists charge you for broken appointments. When the baby is born, there will be a hundred chores crying for your attention (aside from the baby who will probably be crying, too). Diapers, bedclothes, and baby clothes will be on a continual round trip to and from laundering. Formula, bottles, special food, playthings and the baby itself must be maintained on schedule. Babies have to be changed, aired, bathed, turned over, fed and burped with alarming regularity. Cuddling and saying "I'm sorry" may work with a date you've kept waiting for half an hour in the drugstore but cuddling a hungry baby won't make up for a bottle.

A big question in the minds of most teen-age girls is "How do you know when you're pregnant? How do you feel and what's happening inside your body?"

A woman's body has three cavities. The upper or chest cavity; the middle or abdominal cavity; the lower or pelvic cavity. The pelvic cavity contains the Uterus —or Womb—which is shaped like an upside-down pear. It is a hollow organ, quite small, measuring three inches in length, two inches in width and one inch in thickness. On either side of it are the two Ovaries, sex glands the size of a pigeon's egg, which contain thousands of tiny eggs or Ova. Once you've reached Puberty, we believe that one Ovary sends forth a full-blown ripe egg each month, the other Ovary doing the same thing the following month.

Then what happens to this full-blown ripe egg? On

either side of the Uterus are the Fallopian Tubes which have fringelike ends that attract the egg into the tube where it is sometimes fertilized. Remember that the egg can only be fertilized in the tubes and only when there has been intercourse.

Each month, the Uterus has prepared itself to receive the egg, its soft lining becomes congested with blood to feed the egg if it should become fertilized. The Uterus is prepared for this possible conception for about ten days which occurs about roughly halfway between the menstrual periods. This is said to be the time when the body is Fertile—that it is ready to conceive a new being. When no baby is conceived, everything that has been stored in the Uterus is then released in the menstrual flow.

Menstruation is a normal flow of blood occurring regularly every twenty-eight to thirty-five days and lasts anywhere from three to six days. The blood that is lost during this time is clean blood, sterile blood, and despite being called a "flow," it actually amounts to only about four ounces for the entire menstrual cycle. As Dr. Rebecca Liswood and other authorities will tell you, "Menstruation is a normal function. You are not sick. You may bathe, swim, exercise, wash your hair, carry on your life as usual."

Conception, or the start of a baby, can only take place when the male sex organ or Penis has entered the female's Vaginal canal and has released Semen which contains live sperm. The sperm then travels up through the mouth of the Uterus into the Uterus and then into the Fallopian Tubes. If it is the time of the month when an Egg is in the tubes then the live sperm will fertilize it. When this happens, the first indication of pregnancy is missing your menstrual period. Let it be strongly stated that reverse logic does not work here. While you will definitely miss your period when you are pregnant, you can very easily miss your period and not be pregnant. During the teen age, your body is still adjusting itself to maturity and periods are often irregular. Also, illness, travel and emotional problems will often upset the cycle.

But back to pregnancy itself. The period stops because, as we have explained above, the thick lining of the Womb is now needed to nourish the baby. The breasts become heavier and fuller for they are starting to create milk to feed the baby at birth.

As for morning sickness and cravings for crazy foods, there is much theory and counter-theory about them. Some girls don't get sick at all. Others are nauseated every morning but are okay once they are out of bed. Even those who do get sick every morning find that this condition disappears after the third month. Some doctors feel that the power of suggestion has much to do with sickness and cravings. You've heard so much about chomping on a raw apple in the morning or having a wild desire for pickles and chocolate sauce that you feel cheated without them. Other doctors explain morning nausea as a result of the Womb's swelling, causing reflex action, and pressing against the stomach and the intestinal wall. Doctors have no rational explanation for hunger crazes, and feel there's nothing wrong with a bit of self-indulgence.

Because of the growing baby, the body is working overtime and this may result in oily skin and lank hair, which is why many pregnant women wear little make-up and short hair, washed more frequently than usual. Teeth require special vigilance. Girls who have never had a cavity in their lives suddenly have several because calcium needed for the baby's bones may not be sufficiently provided for by the milk they drink.

Putting yourself into the care of an obstetrician or Prenatal Clinic is essential. Your weight and general health will be checked regularly. You will be given exercises and diet advice to keep your weight down and prepare your muscles for the actual delivery. Good digestion is important, too, because any discomfort can make you feel awful.

Your doctor will give you a good idea of when the baby is expected to be born, about nine months after conception. The first signs of the actual birth are a low backache and a discharge of mucus slightly tinged with blood. Then the pains begin. They feel like menstrual pains and start low down in the abdomen. They may start to come every half hour and last a few seconds, gradually becoming more frequent and more severe. When they come every five minutes for one hour, it means the Baby may be about ready.

Always be guided by your doctor as to what to expect in labor. Each mother-to-be is different and will receive individual care and advice. Babies are born head first, usually weighing between six and seven pounds and average nineteen inches long.

For a woman there is no greater feeling of personal satisfaction than having a baby and holding it in her arms, a living, breathing child that she and her husband created.

It is very important to regard the child as *"our* baby" rather than *"my* baby." Your greatest responsibility as a wife and mother is to maintain the completeness of the marriage and to make sure that the father doesn't feel left out of the enlarged household.

These, in essence are what happens physically. But what are the emotional and psychological changes you may expect in yourself and in your relationship with your husband and other people?

Emotionally your marriage should be a happy one before starting a family. Where there is friction, misunderstanding, tension, a child will not bring you together no matter what the busybodies say. Children are not supposed to solve your problems. In fact, they bring along their own problems.

As Dr. Stekel has said, "Children are not substitutes for one's disappointed love. They are not substitutes for one's thwarted ideal in life. Children are not mere material to fill out an empty existence. Children are a responsibility and an opportunity. They are neither playthings nor tools for the fulfillment of parental needs or ungratified ambitions. Children are obligations. They should be brought up so as to become happy human beings."

Another emotional aspect is the balance of affection between you and your husband. He may resent the baby because you spend more time taking care of it than of him. You may resent the baby for a different reason. You may feel saddled with it when your husband spends all of Saturday playing baseball—leaving you to mind "the monster."

The grandparents can become a problem, too. Because you're so young, they don't see how you could possibly be capable of raising an infant. Your mother or mother-in-law may take charge, choosing the baby's diet, clothes, furniture. They are well-meaning and not aware that you will develop capability through guidance. So have a frank talk with them and let them know that you *want* to handle your own responsibility at the same time that you appreciate their love and help.

Socially, parenthood changes your status among your friends whether you want it to or not. Although being married immediately makes you different from the gang at school, you still can enjoy parties, all-day excursions, all sorts of activities and amusements in which the length of time away from home doesn't matter. Once the baby comes, however, your social engagements must give way to parental responsibility. A young couple told me they hadn't been to a movie for two years because a sitter was too expensive. Another couple, whose baby had been sick, were too worried about him to leave him alone. Another admitted that their unmarried teen-age friends thought they were "square" for staying home all the time and going to bed early. "You have to if there's a baby howling for a bottle at 6:00 A.M."

Financially, the addition of one eight-pound baby can become quite a drain on the family pocketbook, and may seem even more so if the mother has been working. When her income stops and the baby's expenses mount, making ends meet may be difficult. What it actually costs in dollars and cents to have and maintain a baby is impossible to break down. As a mother, so much depends on your health, whether you're a member of a medical scheme that covers costs, the part of the country you live in which determines the kind of clothes you need for the baby, the type of carriage, and how lucky you've been in the kinds of gifts you've gotten from family and friends.

Special expenses at the actual time of birth include medication, home nursing care and all of the actual medical and obstetrical attention not covered by insurance.

Then, if you have been working, you must decide whether or not to return to work. Ideally, Daddy should go to work and bring home the money to support the household and Mommy should stay home to raise the children and run the household. But with a young marriage, Daddy's earnings are not very large, rent may be high, furniture and appliances have to be paid for, and Mommy may have to pitch in, too.

If you choose to go back to work, you will feel guilty about depriving your baby of motherly care and affection. The day nursery is a wonderful institution but can't take the place of home. According to Dr. Mary Macaulay, it should only be used in cases of real necessity. "The working mother should try to ensure that there is a deputy in the shape of a grandmother, aunt or neighbor to care for her children when she cannot be there, but she should realize that this is only 'second best.' Many a mother does not appreciate how short are the years of childhood until they are over. Those whose task it is to take care of deprived children understand how deeply they all need the secure background which only is ensured by a happy home."

15

DO YOU HAVE TO
GET MARRIED?

The more frightening a subject, the more jokes there are about it. "Nine seconds pleasure; nine months of pain" sounds pretty funny whispered in the lunchroom, but getting "into trouble" is both terrifying and tragic for the girl involved. It is not the kind of mistake for which you can apologize and then forget. An unmarried pregnancy not only presents the obvious physical hazards but the even more destructive and longer-lasting emotional blows.

If you are in love and have thrown all caution to the winds in your love-making, your constant fear is "getting caught," a game of chance you halfway hope may never point its trembling finger at you. Brooding about pregnancy, counting days, worrying about what would happen *if*—can sometimes bring on the symptoms of pregnancy. Young couples have fearfully eloped only to find months later that the symptoms were false.

The mind can and often does play tricks on you. You read an article about polio and suddenly your leg stiffens. You listen to someone tell about a burst appendix and the next day your right side is killing you and it looks like the hospital for you. The dreaded fear of pregnancy can work the same way. The mind is very susceptible to fear and the body sometimes responds without cause. It could respond far enough to make you skip a menstrual period. You've heard that pregnant women get sick in the morning, have wild cravings for crazy foods, get puffy around the middle. All these things can and may happen to you without pregnancy being the reason.

Let us make two points crystal clear. Petting cannot produce a pregnancy. Sexual pleasure does not produce a pregnancy. While ideally a baby should be the result of deep affection and strong love, the actual conception can only result from sexual intercourse. Doctors' reports tell of many young, unmarried girls who thought they were pregnant and, on examination, proved to be virgins.

The chief confusion is, of course, the slap-happy way in which the so-called facts of life are told. We are neither birds nor bees and the sooner this bit of whimsy is forgotten, the better. As discussed in the preceding chapter, the body carries out its functions in a fairly clinical, mechanical format. What separates human beings from the animals are the emotional and spiritual values which must guide us.

What to do if you think you're pregnant? Or, rather, what *not* to do? Most important, don't take bad advice or try wild remedies. Falling downstairs can break your back. Various pills can only make you sick and won't work anyway. If they did, the unwed mother would be a thing of the past. And don't think you'll be an exception. Life is precious and a newly conceived organism clings as tenaciously as you yourself would.

Before the real panic sets in, turn to someone you trust, preferably a parent, a clergyman or your family doctor. If you can't face this, go to a doctor you don't know. Pregnancy is physical and therefore you can't be "slightly pregnant." You either are or you aren't and the only person who can tell you one way or the other is a doctor.

Then what? If you're not, it would be a good time to have a quiet soul-searching with your boy friend. Try to picture what your lives would be like had you been pregnant. A hasty marriage and immediate responsibility would cut short his schooling or force him to take a job without much future. And you would have to quit school because you couldn't face the music.

One of the saddest phrases in the English language is "If we had only waited. . . ." Waited for sex. Waited to get married. Even a deep, true love can turn bitter if the circumstances aren't right. You and your man are in love. You want to marry in about two years, after you've saved some money and he's settled in a good job. If an unexpected baby pushed you into a premature marriage, the strain of responsibility would ruin what could have been a wonderful life together.

Should your fears be confirmed and you are pregnant, To Marry—or Not Marry is of course the vital question.

If you do marry, you may commit yourself to an unsuitable marriage, unhappy for the parents, disastrous for the child, a marriage that could well end in divorce or separation. Being "trapped" by pregnancy, you might not only hate each other for the mess you're in, you might also despise the innocent child who is here through no fault of its own.

It is not too melodramatic to say that a "have to get married" marriage can literally ruin your life. Even if you end it by divorce, you still have to live with the facts of wasted years, a child dependent on you for love and guidance, and the difficult task of starting life anew with the hope of finding the right husband who will care for you and the baby.

This isn't to say that Shotgun Marriages never work out. They do. When Cynthia became pregnant, she and Billy told their parents who were understandably upset but anxious to help them do the right thing. They decided to marry at once, quietly, and live with Cynthia's parents. Cynthia cried during most of the pregnancy, talked in her sleep, had a difficult delivery. The first three months after the baby was born, Cynthia and Billy barely spoke to each other. Then Bill took a job in another city, did very well and three months later, sent for his family. He had found a small, sunny apartment and Cynthia, with her health restored, the baby adorable and a genuine love for Billy, set to work making the place attractive and providing a happy home. They now have another child and, despite the unhappy beginning, are a devoted family.

On the other hand, what happens if you come to the conclusion that marriage is not a good idea, or if the man in question refuses to marry you? Then the decision is whether to give the child out for adoption, or keep it. Again, this is not a choice between ice cream or fruit salad. Your entire life hangs on it.

Marian had broken her engagement with her boy friend before discovering her pregnancy and decided that marrying him would be a worse mistake than being an unwed mother. Her clergyman helped her to find a suitable clinic and gave her spiritual help through her ordeal. At the clinic she was shown every kindness, with no recrimination for her predicament. "I knew I had done wrong. I didn't need a million people telling me."

Before the baby was born, she agreed not to see it and to have it given at once for adoption. Only the authorities would know who received the infant, and the adopting parents would not know the name of the real mother.

Marian returned to her family home. If neighbors and friends guessed what had happened, she did not enlighten them. She found a job, met new friends and a year and a half later she fell in love with a man in his late twenties. When he asked her to marry him, she told him about the baby, but he said it didn't matter. They are married now and have two fine children.

Elizabeth was determined to keep her baby. The father, who was in the Army, had written coolly when told about the coming event, and even though Elizabeth's mother wanted to order the army authorities to make him marry her, the girl refused to force him into it.

She adored babies and said she didn't care what anyone said, she would keep her child and support him herself.

Living at home with her parents and working all day, the baby gradually became more like a little brother to Elizabeth, with the youthful grandmother more the child's mother. When the baby was three, Elizabeth fell in love and told the man about the baby.

He didn't want to take on another man's child. Fortunately for Elizabeth, her mother was young enough and strong enough to want to raise the child herself.

In yet another case, Carolyn at sixteen had given her baby for adoption but at twenty-nine still had not married. Nervous, fretful, she is afraid of sex. She relives the pain and loneliness of having the baby, dreads the thought of having to go through it again. Men want to marry her but she always finds a reason to refuse. She is fearful of sex because she is haunted by the shame of her pregnancy and the nightmare months that followed.

You may have some vague ideas about terminating the pregnancy by illegal abortion. We talked about abortion in an earlier chapter. We will not go into the moral and religious aspects of the subject here. Fear and despair can often lead the most religious person into a desperate decision. Neither will we go into the pros and cons of abortion and the morality of the law. We must live with the facts, and the chief fact is that abortion is not legal.

You take your life and your sanity in your hands by subjecting your body to unknown, often inept, hands. Because it is illegal, you risk unsanitary conditions and bungling at the mercy of amateurs.

The womb and the ovaries are the most delicate parts of the female anatomy. They can become infected quite easily. You may not be able to have another child because of bungling. You may suffer severe mental anguish leading to a breakdown. You may be sick and listless for months. You may experience such a feeling of horror that you may never be able to marry or allow a man to touch you. As has happened in countless heartbreaking cases, you may die.

In summation, if you think "You Have To Get Married," confirm the fact first. Then the decisions to be made are whether or not to marry and whether or not to keep the child. None of this will be easy; all of this is good reason to keep a tight rein on your emotions and sexual desire before you marry.

The morality of being good before marriage is not only spiritual but logical and practical as well. The more you examine religious teachings of what thou shalt and shalt not do, the more reasonable they seem in terms of modern life.

16

HOW TO BREAK AN ENGAGEMENT

You've made a mistake.

Deep down inside you know it.

It was all so exciting—Easter vacation, the first balmy night of spring, and you sat close together in his car surrounded by star-studded darkness. There were feelings you never felt before, happenings that should not have happened and in the confusion of guilt and happiness that followed, he asked you to marry him and you agreed.

Now you realize that part of your reason for saying yes was that you liked him very much, but a bigger part was the shame of a sexual experience which should rightfully have been part of marriage.

It's May now. You're wearing an engagement ring. Your friends have given you fabulous parties and your old toy chest is stuffed with linens and gadgets for your future home.

Graduation is the third week in June. The wedding is fixed for the following Thursday. The gown, flowers, cake, refreshments have all been ordered. Aside from graduation itself, your wedding is the talk of the school, the preoccupation of all your family and friends.

The last weeks have been a gay round of showers, luncheons, fittings and decisions. But this morning you woke up early and had a long, private think. About graduation. About the future. About the wedding. About marriage and babies.

You're seventeen years old, the world is wide and you suddenly know quite clearly and surely that you don't want to get married for a while. And when you do marry, you know it won't be to your present fiancé.

A moment of clarity is always sobering. A moment of decision brings out the coward in everyone. How to get disengaged? How to unmake all the plans? Pacify all the planners? Explain to your fiancé that the marriage would be a mistake?

However you face the awfulness of it, don't procrastinate. Make the break at once because the closer you get to the wedding day, the harder it becomes to cancel out. There are several ways to handle the situation with dignity. First, of course, he must be told. If you can't bring yourself to face him alone, write him a note saying the wedding is off and inviting him to a meeting with your parents to discuss the best way of making an announcement.

Both families can save face by issuing a joint notice to the newspapers announcing that wedding plans have been canceled by mutual consent.

Keep the news to yourself until it has been made official. Don't say anything to the detriment of your former fiancé that might reflect badly on him. When questioned, say, "We decided we were too young," or "We thought we were rushing into marriage too fast."

It's correct to return all gifts, including the engagement ring.

The worst part about breaking an engagement is the emotional letdown afterward. You know you've done the right thing. You know you'd be sorry if you'd gone through with the wedding. Yet, there is a sad feeling of failure, of wasted time, of people and circumstances not living up to your expectations. Remember, though, however sorry you feel, you would be sorrier still if you went through with the wedding.

Breaking an engagement doesn't necessarily mean you stop seeing your fiancé. It's something for the two of you to discuss. If he's as young as you, he may also have had second thoughts about marriage, and may be just as anxious as you to wait a few years before taking the plunge. You may become fast friends, with the kind of friendship that develops from a shared experience and, as happens in some cases, you may eventually marry.

Socially, your next step is getting back into circulation. Have a big Back-in-Circulation party and invite everyone you know, including old boy friends. To friends and acquaintances who may not have heard about the broken engagement, have an announcement made up that simply says BACK IN CIRCULATION, with your phone number prominently displayed.

Be cautious about one thing. Don't let your new-found freedom push you into promiscuity. Because you are no longer the "property" of one man doesn't mean you have to prove how attractive you are to all comers. Another thing you will find is that your broken engagement will generate a morbid curiosity in lots of men. They will probe you for details, try to worm away your intimate secrets with the argument that "talking it out is good for you."

Talking is good for you but only with someone near and dear whom you can trust. If you don't want your private life a subject for public discussion, make your broken engagement a matter of public record but keep your reasons to yourself.

17

WHAT DO YOU LOOK FOR
IN A MATE?

They say that Opposites Attract. Dark-haired boy flips
over blue-eyed blonde. Country boy goes for city girl.
Shy, indoor type blends with bubbling exhibitionist.

Opposites do attract because each is foreign to the
other. Each has something different in the way of back-

ground, tastes or viewpoint that the other has never known. Is this the basis of friendship? Very much so. But how about marriage? Is there enough foundation on which to build a marriage?

Often it works, but more often the very differences which drew two people together in the first place are what drive them apart later on. Marrying the boy next door is more than a romantic fancy. It makes a great deal of sense. The boy next door shares many of the same cultural and moral standards, many of the same ideals, tastes and customs which most people in your community share.

In the broad sense, what matters to you probably matters to him—and vice versa. How you live, spend your money, furnish your home, raise your children, entertain your friends, plan for the future are all tied up with personal viewpoint.

If you were given a free choice of the qualities you want in a husband, what would they be? Opposites or samenesses? Here is a questionnaire exploring the advantages and disadvantages of "Opposites." It may help you determine the traits most important to you in the man with whom you will spend the rest of your life. Or, if you have already pinned your heart to an "Opposite" you may pick up some tips on coming to terms with your conflicting likes and dislikes.

1. If you love family reunions and he avoids his family like the plague, would you (a) see your family

on the sly without telling him? (b) have your family over whether he liked it or not? (c) stop seeing your family altogether rather than risk an argument?

2. If you want to play records and he wants to read, would you (a) take the record player into another room and play it by yourself? (b) play your records and let him read as best he can? (c) turn off the player and find something to read?

3. If you like to be alone with him and he isn't happy unless there are lots of people around, would you (a) sometimes send him off with the group by himself while you putter around with some lone pursuit? (b) make him spend an evening alone with you—no matter what? (c) go along with him and the mob, feeling very uncomfortable most of the time?

4. If you want a big family and he says "let's wait," would you (a) yearn in silence, keeping up a brave front until he is ready? (b) try to become pregnant anyway and keep your fingers crossed that he'll change his mind? (c) forget about a big family?

5. If you're a Night Person who enjoys staying up late and have to be dragged out of bed in the morning, and he's an Early Bird who folds up with the eleven o'clock news but is bright eyed and bushy tailed at dawn, would you (a) stay up late, sleep late and let him worry about his own breakfast? (b) keep him awake late at night to keep you company, hoping this will make him sleep later in the morning? (c) force yourself to adopt an early-to-bed, early-to-rise routine?

6. If you feel that money should be spent as fast as you get it and he believes in saving, would you (a) charge things and argue about them when the bills come? (b) spend too much, hoping your father will bail you out? (c) work out a spending-and-saving budget according to your income?

7. If your idea of an evening out means dressing up in a cocktail dress and dancing at a club, whereas he thinks ties are torture and considers bowling the height of sophistication, would you (a) suggest places where you can go dancing informally, without a tie? (b) make a tearful scene and insist on the kind of evening you want? (c) learn to enjoy bowling?

The seven situations described may not sound very dramatic yet they are the meat-and-potatoes of living together. By answering honestly, you can have some idea of the ultimate success of your relationship.

If your answers were mostly A, you have a will of your own plus a great talent for compromise, both very important factors in marriage. You realize that married people are not the Bobbsey Twins, that you needn't do everything together, enjoy something simultaneously, face every problem in unison. Knowing how and when to compromise without holding a grudge or feeling disloyal, is an ability that will serve you well in marriage —and in a career, too, for that matter. Be warned, however, that in order to compromise effectively, you must have confidence in yourself, know your own mind, recognize your own needs and serve them as well as your husband.

If your answers were mostly B, you have a strong, demanding personality which will eventually, if not sooner, get you into hot water. You may succeed in forcing someone who loves you to go against his natural instincts and desires to please you. But sooner or later, he will revolt. He cannot go against his nature and training any more than you can completely turn your back on your preferences and upbringing. This forceful attitude can have two results. Either he will fight you tooth and nail on every occasion until petty things trigger a full-scale war. Or, he will knuckle under to you, become a vapid Mr. Milquetoast, saying "Yes, dear" to whatever you wish. Since marriage is neither a battleground nor a struggle for supremacy, predominantly B answers indicate you and the man in question are too Opposite to ever successfully get together.

If your answers were mostly C, you adapt easily, but perhaps a little too much for your own good. You willingly sacrifice your own inclinations, a tendency which leads to martyrdom and growing inner resentment. In some cases, such as the matter of saving, giving in to your partner's wishes means new maturity and an awakened sense of responsibility. In most cases, however, changing yourself completely to suit the wishes of your husband may make you feel righteous and loving for a short period, but soon the delights of self-sacrifice fade and you'll be a seething prisoner of your own making.

From this brief analysis, you can judge some of the implications involved in choosing your mate. For more specific judgment, consider your intended husband in the following terms:

CHARACTER: Honesty. Integrity. Responsibility. Compassion. Tolerance. These are the sum total of a man's character. Does he cheat friends, "put things over" on others, lie his way out of duty? Do you shut your eyes to a shocking lack of compassion, as for instance if you're sick, is he annoyed rather than concerned?

Lack of character comes out in many ways. Borrowing homework in school. Sneaking into movies without paying. Bragging and exaggerating accomplishments. Dragging out a hard-luck story when the chips are down. Using personality as a replacement for work.

Character is far more important than looks, money and a party personality. A good-looking man without loyalty will be too conceited to forego the adoration of other women. A selfish man will spend his money on himself and his own enjoyment, begrudging what he must give to the support of a home. The "life of the party" requires an audience all the time and may turn petulant when you want him to listen to you for a change.

Character can make or break a person. If a man can't keep his word, he won't be able to keep a job or friends or a happy home life. He is the kind of man who will "forget" to pay the rent, "overlook" the telephone bill, "neglect" his job. Convinced the world owes him a living, including you, he operates on the theory of taking without giving.

For your children, you will want a father with strength of character and responsibility to help guide and raise them, a father who will not squander the family income on personal whims, a father and husband who will give you the love and understanding to help you perform your tasks as a wife.

PERSONALITY: Personality runs deeper than mere appeal. You can have a good personality and still have the wrong personality for the person you want to marry. When Ralph doesn't get his own way, he slams doors and refuses to talk. When Helen has to do something disagreeable, she turns cowardly and will hedge or even lie her way out of the situation. When anyone tries to do anything nice for Benjy it's never quite good enough to please him, which can be an intriguing challenge for a short time but palls after a while.

Whiners, grumblers, complainers have vogues of fashion. At the moment they're called Beatniks. If the negative, gloomy outlook of the Beat life appeals to you, remember one thing. Beatniks rarely marry and have only contempt for conventional life. To them, the charm, romance and spiritual flavor of love and marriage are dismissed as square.

AMBITION: When it comes to ambition, you may marry the boy next door, with the same background, schooling, likes and dislikes only to find your goals in life totally at odds. Of course you both want economic security. To you this might mean a small house with enough room for a family, a few personal luxuries and some money in the bank as a margin against error. Your husband may have higher sights, a big house, two cars, outside investments and he may work night and day, depriving you and the children of his presence while he builds up his bank balance.

Socially, you may thrive on parties, joining organizations, broadening your sphere of influence and friendship through social and civic activities. Your husband may not like the round of parties. He may feel you're turning your home into a hotel and resent all intruders. He may prefer camping to the country club, beer parties to champagne.

Where professional and social ambitions are the same, husband and wife can stimulate and encourage each other all the way along the line. You may become a worldly hostess because of your husband's work. His work may prosper from your efforts as a hostess. Be certain that you and your future husband can meet the mutual demands ambitions will make.

18

PREPARATION FOR MARRIAGE

"Me go to a marriage counselor?" exclaimed a young bride-to-be in shocked astonishment. "What for? What do you think I am—neurotic or something?"

Many people—including parents—have the false impression that marriage counseling and professional guidance are solely for people who are popularly called "neurotics"—that is, misfits in society who can't cope with their emotions and need someone to bail them out.

This is definitely not the case! Stated simply, marriage counseling is a professional service whose advice and experience can contribute much to a happy marriage. Marriage counselors are qualified people specially trained in the fields of human relations—what makes people tick, why they do what they do, the pressures and influences of society and how they affect behavior.

Contemporary life has given us much. Independence and freedom from domestic drudgery. Medicines and food for a high level of health. All sorts of packaged meals, gadgets and devices for doing things the easy way.

In other times life was comparatively simple. You didn't buy a dress, you made it. You didn't buy butter, you churned it. You didn't go out on dates at an early age or select your own husband, your parents did it with you, sheltering you through courtship, guiding you into marriage.

It's ironic that expert counseling is sought without question for all the major events in life. If you're job hunting, you go to an employment agency. If you're building a house, you go to an architect. If you're taking a trip, you talk it over with a travel expert.

Ideally, of course, your parents should be your marriage counselors. But often their personal concern for you is so intense that they are unable to view your needs and desires objectively. Don't blame parents too much for this inability. Modern life is complex. There are emotional factors which go very deep and spread very wide. Everything from employment to military service to atomic war have an unsettling effect on all our thoughts and psychological reactions.

Because of all this, every young couple planning to marry should make some effort to consult beforehand with an impartial expert. Far from being "neurotic," this is as sensible a course to take as studying the recipe before you bake a cake. The Scout motto "Be Prepared" was never so apt as when applied to marriage.

Where, then, should you turn?

Many high schools have courses in Family Living, often in the senior year, but frequently they are of a general nature designed as an approach to the subject without dwelling on your specific case.

Your family doctor may be all the marriage counselor you need. When you go to him for your premarital examination and the blood test needed for your marriage license, you and your fiancé should discuss with him the physical and emotional aspects of marriage and family life. If there are some intimate questions you want to ask privately, request a few minutes alone before or after your joint meeting. Your doctor knows the kind of person you are, your emotional fears, your physical weaknesses, and can anticipate as well as offset problems.

Then there are your religious leaders. Obviously you will tell your minister that you are planning marriage. More than likely he will recommend a Marriage Preparation Course if there is one in your locality, or a Marriage Clinic under the auspices of a hospital, university or your religious organization itself.

Before going to a Marriage Counselor, inquire first as to the professional background and training of the person recommended. There is no law requiring a marriage counselor to carry a license, so you owe it to your future happiness to check credentials.

One good way to find a suitable marriage counselor is to look under "Social Service Agencies" in your telephone book or write to either the American Association of Marriage Counselors or The Family Service Association of America. The addresses of these and other worthwhile groups offering information and service are listed at the end of this chapter.

Nothing is too "silly" to bring to a marriage counselor. You have nightmares about sex. You're convinced you'll die in childbirth. You think you're pregnant right now. You don't want to finish school but you want to earn some money. You hate your parents but wish you didn't. You lean too much on your mother. You're engaged and want to break it off but haven't the nerve. You have a "bad reputation" and want to change but don't know how to get out of the rut. You feel very sexy and wonder if you're a nymphomaniac.

In addition to the questions you want to ask, there

may be some you haven't even thought to consider. And by this, I don't mean you should go out looking for problems. For instance, one social service agency tells of a teen-age couple who had been coming to them for discussion and then turned up one day—married. When asked where they were going to spend the night, they had no idea! They hadn't thought that far ahead.

Except for special discussion of unusual personal problems you may have, what can you expect to happen when you go to see a marriage counselor?

At the Marriage Consultation Center, Community Church, New York City, you and your future husband are interviewed together, with separate discussions for more personal matters held at another time. According to the procedure established by the pioneer sociologist Dr. Abraham Stone, the discussion covers the three major objectives of marriage: 1. the security of love and mutual belonging; 2. sexual fulfillment; 3. home and family. Counseling helps you to achieve these, by helping you to understand the emotional and physical requirements of each.

An hour's counseling along these lines before the wedding may be more valuable than weeks of counseling later when difficulties have arisen. In fact forewarned is forearmed and you may avoid many difficulties.

Love is always first on the list for discussion. Love is essential to marriage but it must be mature love, a genuine "caring" for one another. In addition to loving one another, you should also both like the same things.

Shared activities, experiences and ideas make a firm footing for marital happiness.

With love comes sex and reproduction. The Marriage Consultation Center uses drawings, diagrams and plastic models to show the structure and functions of the sex organs, sperm and egg formation. The process of conception, childbearing and childbirth are clearly shown to clear up any vague notions or secret misapprehensions.

Love-making comes into the discussion, too. Although petting and love-making before marriage are exciting, the experts reveal from their vast experience that in most cases, satisfactory married sex life may take months to achieve. They caution you that your honeymoon may not be as sexually sublime as expected —and for very ordinary reasons. After weeks of nerves, preparations, parties and the like, you're both physically and emotionally exhausted! By understanding this, you won't be too worried and you'll know why.

According to Dr. Eleanor Hamilton, a well-known psychologist and member of the American Association of Marriage Counselors, "In premarital counseling, we say that the success of a marriage depends not so much on the ability of each partner to meet the other's *conscious* needs, but on their respective capacities to meet each other's *unconscious* needs. It involves encouraging into consciousness the hopes, dreams and longings of your lover that lie hidden—even from himself."

Communication is the first step. "Good communication," says Dr. Hamilton, "is nourishment for the spirit.

Bad communication is poison that eventually will kill all love between marital partners."

Sexual preparedness is second. "In our culture we talk a lot about sex—often pornography. Ours is the most pornographic culture on earth and at the same time one of the most sexually inhibited. Professional counseling can help overcome emotional as well as physical perplexities."

Religion comes into it, too, as well as the influences of family, in-laws and the management of money. You may never have crystallized your religious convictions in talks with your fiancé—even if you are of the same faith. You may feel tied to your family's authority, worried about your parents' influence and yet never discuss these things openly. Money is frequently considered "not quite nice" to talk about, as if cold, hard cash might somehow destroy the romantic illusion of love. On the contrary, money troubles are often the chief cause of quarrels and resentment in marriage.

How many times should you go? The counselor will advise you according to your own needs. Several experts agreed that a series of five is suggested as best, with the bride and groom seen separately and then together.

One of the best things about marriage counseling is that you usually find a friend for life. Couples who have been happily married for years consider their counselor a part of the family, someone to call on in time of stress, someone who will want to know all their triumphs too.

What does premarital counseling cost? Courses in high school are generally part of the curriculum. Courses elsewhere, such as the "Preparation for Marriage" program at New York's Y.M.C.A., cost two-fifty for a session of six classes. Individual counseling varies, with fees based on a sliding scale depending on your ability to pay. As Mrs. Shirley Camper of the Family Service Association of America explained, "By ability to pay, we are not concerned with total income so much as the family demands on that income. For instance, if the family income is $8,000 but there are five children to take care of, the ability to pay for counseling is on a par with families earning less. Nobody is ever turned away at any of our member agencies due to inability to pay. Some agencies do have waiting lists however, and it would be wise to be prepared for a wait."

How to select your premarital counseling?

First of all, there are courses in premarital education, some avaliable, as noted elsewhere in this chapter, in high school. If it is unavailable at your school, inquire at your local Y.M.C.A., or Y.M.H.A. to see if they have such instruction. Most do. Or write to the Home and Family Life Department of the university nearest you and ask if they have an extension department open to the public.

Every Catholic Archdiocese has a Family Life Bureau for consultation. Most Protestant and Jewish groups make marriage preparation available through their pastors or rabbis and other trained leaders.

The "Yellow Pages" of the telephone book list Social Service Agencies and a phone call will put you in touch with the proper person.

In addition, here are the names and head office addresses of the leading associations of marriage counselors. Write to one or several for information about the most suitable agency near your home. Address your letter to the Executive Secretary. It's courteous to enclose a stamped self-addressed envelope for your reply.

MARRIAGE COUNSELING SERVICE OF GREATER NEW YORK, 1 Nevins Street, Brooklyn 1, N. Y.

THE AMERICAN ASSOCIATION OF MARRIAGE COUNSELORS, 27 Woodcliff Drive, Madison, New Jersey.

PLANNED PARENTHOOD FEDERATION OF AMERICA, INC., 501 Madison Avenue, New York 22, N. Y.

CANADIAN WELFARE COUNCIL, 55 Parkdale Avenue, Ottawa 3, Ontario, Canada.

FLORENCE CRITTENTON HOMES ASSOCIATION, INC., 608 South Dearborn Street, Chicago 5, Illinois.

MARGARET SANGER BUREAU, 17 West 16 Street, New York 11, N. Y.

FAMILY SERVICE ASSOCIATION OF AMER-
ICA, 215 Park Avenue South, New York 3, N. Y.
(Member agencies are in almost all states and in
Canada.)

TAMPAX EDUCATIONAL DEPT., 161 East 42
Street, New York 17, N. Y. (Write for booklets
plus schedule of lectures in various parts of the
country.)

Perhaps the whole reason for seeking out a marriage
counselor before marriage can be summed up in one
word: KNOWLEDGE.

If you know what to expect, you can prepare for it
together, help each other over the rough spots, handle
each obstacle as it arises and enjoy the confidence and
contentment that comes with knowing what you're
doing.

As stated in the Book of Proverbs, "The lips of
knowledge are a precious jewel."

19

SOME DEFINITIONS— A GLOSSARY OF TERMS

I think college dictionaries make a grave mistake in omitting words that have to do with sexual intercourse and reproduction, words that have only become secretive and shameful because their meaning and usage are clouded with obscene implications.

Sexual intercourse is not obscene.

Reproduction is not obscene.

The human body and how it works is not obscene.

Here are some words and phrases you may have heard or used yourself without a clear and concise knowledge of their meaning.

ABORTION: The termination of a pregnancy, usually in the early stages. There are two different types. One is called Spontaneous Abortion—or Miscarriage —meaning that the baby being formed inside the womb has become dislodged and discharged from the body in the same way as the menstrual period.

A medical abortion, that is, the surgical removal of the unborn baby by a doctor, is illegal in the United States, except in rare cases where the doctor asserts that the mother's life is in danger.

Otherwise, abortion by doctors—or anyone else—is a criminal act subject to long imprisonment. We will not question these laws, nor go into the religious aspects of preventing a birth. The danger of abortion lies in its shadiness, the physical hazards of unsanitary conditions and crackpot or amateur "doctors," the emotionl risks of a mental breakdown and the grim possibility of death from infection. In countless cases, women who have had abortions have been unable to have children.

CAESAREAN BIRTH: A kind of birth in which the baby is delivered by surgical operation. A Caesarean is performed when the doctor concludes that a normal birth would injure or kill either the mother or the baby. Regarded as a simple operation such as an appendectomy, a Caesarean means cutting through the abdomen and into the uterus—or womb—and removing the baby. The Caesarean is performed at about the time the baby is expected, not before. The name goes back to Julius Caesar who is said to have been born this way. Caesarean birth is relatively easy, and the mother recovers within a few days. Notable Caesarean mothers are Elizabeth Taylor and Jacqueline Kennedy.

CONCEPTION: When the Egg—or Ovum—inside the tubes is fertilized by the male Sperm during intercourse, and a baby begins to grow, the mother is said to conceive.

CONTRACEPTION: Preventive measures against conception. There are many methods to be discussed with your doctor if you are interested.

EJACULATION: Muscular ejection of sperm together with prostatic and seminal fluid which comes in spurts from the urethral canal of the penis.

FRIGIDITY: Sexually unresponsive or "cold." Usually, this term is applied to women because physically, a female is able to have sexual intercourse without responding, something a male cannot do. Frigidity is not physical. It is purely mental or emotional and may come from a deep-rooted fear of sex or disgust with the body that is a holdover from childhood training. You can deeply love a man, ardently want to express this love in physical terms yet still recoil from sex. If a husband is understanding, he will talk to his wife about her fears; be romantic in his attitudes; make her feel wanted and needed; indulge her with all of his love; try to help her get rid of her wrong indoctrination into sex and the sex act. If he fails, then she needs the help of a psychiatrist.

GENITALS: Sex organs, both male and female.

GESTATION: The period of time during which the baby grows inside the mother. In humans, this is about nine months.

GYNECOLOGIST: A doctor who specializes in the study and treatment of women's diseases and disorders, especially those of the reproductive organs. Usually a Gynecologist is also an obstetrician.

HETEROSEXUAL: A person with sexual desire for the opposite sex.

HOMOSEXUAL: Simply put, a person with sexual desire for the same sex.

HYMEN: A thin membrane that usually covers the entrance of the vagina. Extremely elastic and easily stretched, its being intact was once considered the test of a girl's virginity, but the active sports lives of girls today usually means the hymen is broken before the first sexual experience. In extremely rare instances, where the first sexual experience is difficult, it may be necessary to have a doctor penetrate the hymen, a quick and painless process.

IMPOTENCE: The inability of the male to perform the sex act. This is thought to be psychic rather than physical.

INTERCOURSE (mating): The entry of the male penis into the female vaginal canal and the release of sperm is the clinical description of a life experience that should combine all the emotional expression and fulfillment of love.

MISCARRIAGE: The body's ejection of a baby which is not developed enough to be able to live.

OBSTETRICIAN: A doctor who specializes in the care and treatment of women during pregnancy, delivers the baby and cares for the mother for the first three months afterward.

ORGASM: The climax of sexual sensation during intercourse.

OVULATION: Expulsion of the full-blown ripe egg from the Ovary into the pelvic cavity. This happens once during each month.

PENIS: Male sex organ.

PREGNANCY: This is the period of forty weeks in which a sperm-fertilized Ovum about the size of a pin-head develops into a baby. The Ovum travels down its Fallopian tube and enters the Uterus. There it begins to grow. At the end of the first month, it is a quarter inch in size, a month later it is three-quarters of an inch. In this early stage, it is called an Embryo. At four months, five inches long and with a definitely human form, the name changes to Fetus. At the end of nine months, the baby is born through the vagina.

PROMISCUOUS: Simply means "indiscriminate." Promiscuous behavior shows an uncaring lack of self-respect or respect for others. This unfortunate attitude can express itself in your wardrobe and your friendships as well as in sexual experience. The opposite of Promiscuous is Selective. A person who is selective—or choosy—always holds out for the best, and generally gets it.

PUBERTY: The stage when a child develops into a growing adult. It takes place at different ages in different young people and manifests itself by menstruation in girls and nocturnal emissions in boys. Boys' arms and legs grow longer. Girls' bodies become rounder. A chemical substance from the base of the brain comes down through the blood stream and notifies the sex glands to produce the hormones and other properties needed for reproduction.

SEMEN: Male fluid containing spermatic fluid, prostatic fluid and sperm.

SPERM: Microscopic male seed contained in semen (or seminal fluid) which is ejaculated from the penis during intercourse.

STERILITY: The inability to conceive a child.

UMBILICAL CORD: The connection between the mother and the unborn baby through which blood vessels carry nourishment to the child and remove waste products from the child. At birth, its usefulness over, it is tied and cut. This does not hurt the mother any more than cutting her nails or her hair. The part that was attached to the baby becomes the navel.

UTERUS: Another word for womb, a hollow organ in the female body which houses the fertilized Ovum while it grows into a baby.

VD: Veneral Diseases such as syphillis or gonorrhea, which are not only destructive to the bodies of the parents but almost always will result in miscarriage or an unhealthy offspring. While VD is generally contracted through sexual intercourse, it may also be caught in other ways, or inherited. Most states require blood tests before the issuance of a marriage certificate in order to assure freedom from VD.

WOMB: See Uterus.